ENZO BIANCHI was born in Castel
Boglione, Piedmont, Italy, in 1943. In 1965,
after graduating from the University of
Turin, he founded an ecumenical monastic
community—the Bose Community—of
which he is still the prior. Friar Bianchi is a
well-known author of books on *lectio divina*
and the spiritual life, which have been
translated into many languages. He has
dedicated himself to the search for spirituality capable of giving life to Christians
today and furthering communion among all
people.

The Bose Community now numbers
over eighty brothers and sisters of various
Christian traditions, and receives thousands
of visitors annually.

ALSO AVAILABLE BY THE AUTHOR IN THIS SERIES PUBLISHED BY
PARACLETE PRESS:

Echoes of the Word (2013)
God, Where Are You? (2014)

LECTIO DIVINA

From God's Word to Our Lives

Enzo Bianchi

Foreword by Rowan Williams

PARACLETE PRESS

BREWSTER, MASSACHUSETTS

2015 First Printing This Edition

Lectio Divina: From God's Word to Our Lives

ISBN 978-1-61261-642-1

Translated by Christine Landau

First published in Great Britain in 2015 by Society for Promoting Christian Knowledge, 36 Causton Street, London SW1P 4ST, www.spckpublishing.co.uk.

Original Italian version published in Italy in 2008 as *Ascoltare la Parola: Bibbia e Spirito: la 'lectio divina' nella chiesa* by Edizioni Qiqajon, Comunità di Bose

Library of Congress Cataloging-in-Publication Data
Bianchi, Enzo.
  [Ascoltare la Parola. English]
  Lectio divina : from God's word to our lives / Enzo Bianchi ; foreword by Rowan Williams.
     pages cm
  Includes bibliographical references.
  ISBN 978-1-61261-642-1
  1. Bible—Devotional use. 2. Prayer—Christianity. I. Title.
  BS617.8.B5113 2015
  248.3—dc23   2014045199

10 9 8 7 6 5 4 3 2 1

This edition published by Paraclete Press
Brewster, Massachusetts
www.paracletepress.com

Printed in the United States of America

CONTENTS

PART ONE
BIBLE AND SPIRIT

PART TWO
LECTIO DIVINA IN THE CHURCH

FOREWORD

To read Enzo Bianchi's work is, among other things, to be forcefully made aware that we have got used to a rather thin diet of resources to help us read the Bible. We have plenty of good scholarship and plenty of good popular summaries of that scholarship—but very little on the actual *theology* of reading the Bible, very little on reading the Bible as a central form of our *discipleship*.

Twentieth-century theology has left us with a great heritage of recovering and reworking some of the major themes in the kind of scriptural study practiced in the early or medieval Church or in the Reformation: Henri de Lubac, Karl Barth, and others have helped us question the bland modern assumption that the Bible is primarily a set of historical texts, to be read and understood by criteria external to themselves. All but the narrowest of conservative Protestant theology has moved some distance away from that other modern assumption that sees Scripture as a guaranteed source of unquestionably reliable information and little more. But how then should we understand the relationship between our common life and prayer and our study of Scripture?

Br. Enzo often returns in one way or another to the theme of "epiclesis"—the invocation of the Holy Spirit—as a focal act of the community, especially the monastic community. It is part of the way in which we live as Christians with a keen awareness of the age to come, the way we live eschatologically. And what the Holy Spirit does is to bring us face to face with the Word of God, the living action of the Second Person of the Trinity. Thus if we read Scripture as we must, invoking the Holy Spirit, what we encounter in Scripture is that living Word. We are made contemporary with what Scripture witnesses to; we discover the *unity* of Scripture not in any theory but in the person of Jesus Christ, on whom the whole of Scripture converges and around whom it finds its shape.

For Br. Enzo, this is the key to an extraordinarily broad range of reflection—on priesthood, on religious life, on the challenges of contemporary European society, on the daily struggle and frustration of being a Christian. If it is true that there is no way of finding or being found by God that is not also a finding of one's own humanity, then what is happening in the scriptural encounter is an unveiling of who we are—as human beings and as the particular people we happen to be. In this encounter we meet the God who has already become present in us and seeks to be made known through us; we become a place where God's glory can be manifest. The variety of scriptural narrative is testimony to the diversity of the modes of God's presence in each one. So as we read, in community, in company with our brothers and sisters, we are doubly alert—to what we are being taught about the calling, dignity, and destiny of men and women, and to what we are learning about our own calling and gifting.

The reading of Scripture is a genuinely sacramental event, one in which God's act in the past, the present, and the future is laid bare to us and in which we are ourselves caught up in that act. As we absorb the communication of the Word, we become contemporary with the events of primal revelation, and contemporary with the climax of history in which Christ is all in all. And it is in this way alone that we become truly contemporary with our own times. We may think there is no problem about being "contemporary" here and now; but the truth is that, without an anchorage in the Word of God, we are insubstantial, distracted by our own private agendas and incapable of truthful relationship with each other. Our communion with God the Word, realized in our communion as readers together of the written vehicle of the Word, delivers us from this shadow world and equips us to give voice to something of God's perspective on the world we inhabit—both as celebrants of the environment in which we stand and as hopeful critics of a human world that is profoundly confused and conflicted.

Br. Enzo's books are a powerful witness to what the monastic calling can still make possible in our time. Behind all he writes stands the practice of the community at Bose, a community that has offered a unique remodeling of the traditions of classical monasticism in a style that is compelling for countless people today. It is a community in which the corporate study of Scripture is central; those who have experienced biblical reflection in community at Bose will know what an extraordinary experience it is, an opening of unimagined depths in the text. But the friends and guests of Bose will also recognize how this approach shapes the whole ethos of worship through a liturgy that, like all the best monastic liturgies, lays out the wholeness of scriptural imagery and narrative in all its rich interconnection and interdependence. Br. Enzo's writing shows how this, far from creating an inward-looking, "aesthetic" spirit, provides the resources we need as Christians to bring real illumination to the confusions of our culture.

Enzo Bianchi is one of the most significant Christian voices in Europe. He shows what can be achieved by an immersion in Scripture that involves both intellect and imagination alike, and—in common with all the most serious Christian voices of our day—he cannot be labeled as a partisan "liberal" or "traditionalist." He offers exactly what the monastic voice at its truest has always offered: a way into the heart of our ecclesial and social questions that is honest, patient, and sensitive. His is a perspective that the English-speaking Christian world should welcome enthusiastically.

Rowan Williams
Magdalene College, Cambridge

INTRODUCTION

With these few elementary notes on *lectio divina*, we hope to have provided readers with an opportunity to renew or develop a taste for a way of reading Scripture which is as old as the church itself, and which has deep roots in Judaism. I don't think we've said anything new. We've simply made a quick review of the patristic and monastic traditions, which made *lectio divina* a form of daily nourishment within the context of praying the opus Dei, the Liturgy of the Word.[1]

This is how I ended my book *Praying the Word: an Introduction to Lectio Divina* almost forty years ago. The biblical movement and liturgical reform supported by the Second Vatican Council had recently ended the "exile" of God's Word from the daily lives of Catholics, and the book came out of my reflection on those events. It has had a lasting success I did not expect, both in Italy (where it is now in its twenty-third edition) and abroad (it has been translated into some twenty languages, including Russian, Greek, Korean, and Japanese). Another motivation to write came from the fact that I was living in community, an experience that changed me profoundly. Six brothers and I were in the process of making a life commitment to follow Christ in celibacy and common living, and we were creating a monastic community centered around the Word of God. In the book, I was bold in ways that only a young and inexperienced writer can be, but I had no desire to develop any particular theories. I simply wanted to share intuitions that have been at the heart of the everyday Christian experience for a very long time.

In the intervening years, I have had no shortage of opportunities to explore all the nuances of the topic. I am still living out the same monastic adventure, and *lectio divina* continues to be part of my daily personal prayer. I feel that I have been able to grasp—purely by grace, in the poverty of my daily search for God's will—the truth of a patristic saying that was made famous by Gregory the Great: *Divina eloquia cum legente crescent* (Scripture grows together with the person reading it). Whenever I write or speak on how to read God's Word, I always seek—whether in the church fathers or in contemporary writers, in medieval mystics or in the Reformers—my one true passion of seeing how words on a page can bring us into the presence of the Word made flesh.

About fifteen years ago, I had a memorable opportunity to revisit this topic. I was invited by the former Cardinal Ratzinger to edit a volume on Christian biblical exegesis with him and with Fr. Ignace de la Potterie. The result of our stimulating conversation was a book we presented together to the Gregorian University and the Pontifical Biblical Institute.[2] This was a unique experience, but I have also kept up a ministry of the word in my monastic community and elsewhere. I have interacted with every sort of church group imaginable, from rural parishes to missionaries serving in Africa and Asia, from people attending Bible meetings in European capitals to members of silent religious communities where I have led retreats. All of these experiences have confirmed my basic conviction that in *lectio divina*, in Scripture, we can truly meet the one who speaks, the living Word, God himself. When we read prayerfully, we draw out of the biblical text the living word that calls us to live full and rich Christian lives, even if that word's work in us remains mysterious.

We need *lectio divina* today more than ever. All around us are forms of religious expression and attraction to the divine in which words like "God" or even "Jesus Christ" are at risk of being emptied out and refilled with our own projections and desires. At times we need to ask whether the God in whom Christians believe and of whom they speak is actually the living God revealed by Jesus, whose humanity explains, reveals, and tells God's story, or whether we are dealing with a God who is the product of human dreams and hopes. It is essential to listen carefully to Scripture, interpret it, and pray it so that we may come to know God truly, and so that our engagement with him results in a celebration of covenant.

Lectio divina can veer down a number of false paths when it turns away from the tradition of the universal church. People may read Scripture in search of a simple emotional experience and not understand how thoroughly the Bible is grounded in history and culture. On the other side of the spectrum is fundamentalism, an attachment to the "letter that kills" rather than to the "Spirit who gives life." Because these tendencies are very common, I have returned again and again over the years to the all-important relationship between *lectio divina* and the church's life. This relationship is so fundamental that Benedict XVI chose it as the topic for an upcoming bishops' synod.

xiv | *Lectio Divina*

I hope that these pages may be heard as a simple yet faithful echo of my personal experience, my community's path and my journey with the church. For years, I have broken the bread of the Word for the brothers and sisters in my community. Much of what I say here comes from that experience. It also comes from many years of preaching the Word to listeners from all walks of life. I would like to see this book ultimately as no more than a small gesture of gratitude to those witnesses of the Word whom the Lord has allowed me to meet, those "martyrs" of faith who have found ways to express all the richness of the gospel in their lives. Only those people who put God's Word into practice have really heard it. They are the ones who truly understand the biblical text, because they obey without delay the word Christ never tires of speaking to us. The *sequential sancti evangelii* for today—today's gospel—is not the product of brilliant scholarly research. It is the life and witness of God's holy people, those who are faithful disciples of the Word made flesh, their Lord.

ENZO BIANCHI
Prior of the Monastery of Bose
September 3, 2008
FEAST DAY OF ST. GREGORY THE GREAT
A POPE PASSIONATE ABOUT SCRIPTURE

PART ONE

BIBLE AND SPIRIT

CHAPTER 1

THE ROOMS AND THE KEYS

The Hebrew has passed on a beautiful tradition to us; it has to do with divine Scripture in its entirety. According to this man, all of divinely inspired Scripture, because of the obscurity that is in it, can be compared to many locked rooms in a house. Next to each room is a key, but it is not the key for that room. The keys are all distributed next to the rooms, but none of them matches the room near which it is placed. The Hebrew says that it is a very difficult task to find the keys and match them with the doors they will open. Similarly, we come to understand the Scriptures that are obscure precisely when we start by placing them alongside one another, because they have their own interpretive principle hidden in their midst. I think the Apostle also suggests a similar method for understanding the divine words when he says: *We speak of these things in words not taught by human wisdom but taught by the Spirit, comparing spiritual things with spiritual things* (1 Cor. 2:13).[3]

This is how the third-century church father Origen expresses the cornerstone of his own approach to biblical exegesis, and of any spiritual interpretation of Scripture: *Scriptura sui ipsius interpres*—Scripture is its own interpreter.

The keys to understanding Scripture, for Origen, are found in Scripture itself. This statement has two implications: that the Bible is a unity, and that it is inspired—meaning that the Bible's words are Spirit-bearing, "Spirit and life" (John 6:63). They bear the Spirit's *dynamis* or power, so that the knowledge we gain from Scripture is the Spirit's teaching. We know because it has been revealed (cf. Matt. 11:25–27). This is why only "the one who has the key of David" (Rev. 3:7) can open the locked doors. "The Root of David" alone (Rev. 5:5) can break open the seals of the book. The One who inspired the holy texts is the only one who can unveil their meaning.[4]

If we want to understand the Bible, we will see it not only as an object to grasp, but also as a subject. We enter into a relationship based on mutuality and dialogue, and this is why the biblical text is able to inspire, make meaning, and be useful for salvation (cf. 2 Tim. 3:15–16). The Bible's unique status calls for the interpreter to use an approach uniquely suited to it. Faith is the space in which we meet and come to know a text that was born of faith. Our faith then becomes hermeneutical potential, a key that opens the door to knowing Christ as we spend time in dialogue with Scripture.

Even when a passage of the Bible is obscure, Origen says that faith is where we should begin:

> First of all, believe, and you will find great and holy use-fulness beneath what you thought was an obstacle.[5]

When we have faith, a stumbling block in the text may turn into something that is revelatory—and then our faith opens into thanksgiving. Origen points out on the basis of a passage from Romans (9:20–21) that Scripture does not necessarily answer each and every question we ask of it. What happens when people read the Bible today, he explains, is similar to what happened during Jesus's lifetime: "Those who were . . . faithlessly inquiring of the Lord by what authority he was doing the things he was doing . . . were not even deemed worthy of an answer."[6]

But when Daniel the prophet, a faithful and attentive servant, questioned God because he

> . . . desired to know the will of the Lord, for which he was even named "man of desires," it was not said to him, "Who are you?" But an angel was sent to teach him about all God's ways and judgments. Therefore, if there is some secret and hidden thing of God we long to know, if we are men of desires and not contentions, let us faithfully and humbly inquire into the more concealed judgments of God that are sown in the Holy Scriptures. Surely this is also why the Lord was saying, "Search the Scriptures!" since he knew that these things are opened not by those who fleetingly listen to or read [the Scriptures] while occupied with other business, but by those who with an upright and sincere heart search more deeply into the Holy Scriptures, by constant effort and uninterrupted nightly vigils.[7]

Who is the reader whom Scripture hopes to find? For Origen, it is a man or woman who is *desiring, not contentious*, a person who truly wants to know God, love and cling to God, and do the divine will. Origen's words are consistent with Scripture's own desire in our regard, at least insofar as this purpose and intention is voiced by the scriptural self-awareness we find in the original ending of the Fourth Gospel. In John 20:31 we read:

> These [signs] are written so that you may come to believe that Jesus is the Messiah, the Son of God, and that through believing you may have life in his name.

Scripture beckons to the reader to become personally involved, appealing to his or her faith. Interpretation seen in this light becomes a meeting of desires.

There are a number of other principles that make up Origen's richly nuanced exegetical method. One of them is the idea that the biblical text has multiple senses. Origen bases this idea on Proverbs 22:20 and fleshes it out in analogy to the traditional anthropological conception of the self as threefold (body, soul, and spirit). According to this interpretive principle, there are three senses—literal, moral, and spiritual—concealed in the words of Scripture.

Another principle is derived from 1 Corinthians 10:6–11 ("These things happened to them to serve as an example, and they were written down to instruct us"). The idea here is that we must discover how the biblical text is relevant in our lives today. And then there is Origen's very important conviction that Truth is mystery. Because of this, Truth—the Word, God's Son—cannot be fully captured in the written word, but goes beyond it. In commenting on the second ending of the Fourth Gospel (". . . there are also many other things that Jesus did; if every one of them were written down, I suppose that the world itself could not contain the books that would be written," John 21:25), Origen glimpses an unsaid, unwritten dimension in the Bible that reveals mystery:

> Not only is it impossible for the grandeur of reality to be set down in writing, it cannot even be spoken by a fleshly tongue, nor can it be expressed in human words and languages.[8]

Both the Bible's words and its silences are revelatory of the One who is "the Word come forth from silence." Scripture wants to introduce the reader to *this* Word. This is why Origen says, "I think that all of the Scriptures together, even when they are understood perfectly and in depth, are only the very first elements and the briefest of introductions to the totality of knowledge."[9] Still, only Scripture, when encountered in the Holy Spirit, has the ability to guide the reader beyond itself, into what is "beyond the written" (cf. 1 Cor. 4:6). There is only one way to reach this knowledge, and that is to let oneself be caught up in the Spirit's action and go where the Spirit goes.

> It is not granted to everyone to seek what is "beyond the written"—the only way is to become one with it.[10]

With its words and silences, Scripture wants to guide readers to a way of knowing Christ that is the Spirit's work and the fruit of spiritual interpretation. Why else would Scripture itself tell readers that the Holy Spirit is its own hermeneutical key? It is the gift of the Spirit that gives Jesus's disciples insight into the words he has spoken, and into scriptural words (cf. John 2:22, 7:39, 14:26). The Spirit is also the interpreter of what Christ left unspoken, inspiring his disciples throughout history to be faithful to the Gospel in creative, not literal or legalistic, ways. As Jesus says in the Gospel of John:

> I still have many things to say to you, but you cannot bear them now. When the Spirit of truth comes, he will guide you into all the truth; for he will not speak on his own, but will speak whatever he hears, and he will declare to you the things that are to come. He will glorify me, because he will take what is mine and declare it to you. (John 16:12–14)

And so "the Scriptures wish to be read in the same Spirit in which they were written, and through the Spirit they must be understood."[11]

CHAPTER 2

IS A SPIRITUAL
APPROACH TO THE BIBLE
RELEVANT TODAY?

I have spoken about Origen at some length because he is the classic representative of a tradition of interpretation that "was the formula for Christian biblical exegesis as it was practiced without interruption until the sixteenth century, when the critical era turned it into simply one possible way of reading the Bible."[12] Origen reminds us that reading Scripture can be "a complete exegetical act, one which integrates textual, liturgical, and existential realities that are often weakened today by their mutual isolation."[13]

Several decades ago, a heated debate took place over how the Bible ought to be interpreted in the Catholic Church. The place of scholarly exegesis in the Church was an especially contested topic. An urgent need was felt to re-unify exegesis: to rediscover what it means to read Scripture spiritually, to return the Bible to its place at the heart of spirituality, and to do exegesis so that it is also theology. It was also felt that homiletics, catechesis, Christian initiation, and the Church's *traditio fidei* all ought to be biblically grounded. Exegesis, many realized, needs to be brought close to people's daily lives so that it can lead to prayer and action.

More recently, we have realized that we need to make a careful distinction between healthy spiritual exegesis and ways of reading the Bible that are overly spiritualized, allegorical, literal, or fundamentalist.

My conviction is that the need to read Scripture in the Spirit flows naturally from the Bible's centrality in the life of the Church. It is a task on which the Church's present and future hinge.

THE BIBLE AT THE HEART
OF THE CHURCH

The Bible's centrality in the Church, which Catholics rediscovered during the Second Vatican Council after having lost sight of it for quite some time, is expressed in the conciliar document *Dei Verbum*. This document affirms that Scripture unifies the four major areas of the Church's life. In *liturgy*, the Bible "make[s] the voice of the Holy Spirit sound again and again," and through it "the Father . . . comes lovingly to meet his children, and talks with them" (*DV* 21). *Preaching* should be "nourished and ruled by sacred scripture" (*DV* 21). *Theology* must be based "on the written word of God . . . . as its permanent foundation," and the study of Scripture "should be the very soul of sacred theology" (*DV* 24). As for *the faithful in their daily lives*, they should "immerse themselves in the scriptures by constant spiritual reading" (*DV* 25).

The Word wants to renew the face of the Church by turning every Christian into its servant (cf. Lk. 1:12), and every ministry into a ministry of the Word (Acts 20:20). "Pastoral preaching, catechetics and all forms of Christian instruction, among which the liturgical homily should hold pride of place," (*DV* 24) need to look to the Bible for their nourishment and vitality. The Bible is at the heart of the Church so that, by keeping it close to us, we can learn "the surpassing knowledge of Jesus Christ" by frequent reading: "Ignorance of the scriptures is ignorance of Christ" (*DV* 25). Christianity is "not the religion of the Bible, but the religion of Jesus Christ."[14] This means that it is not a religion of the Book but a "religion of interpretation."[15] The Bible's centrality in Christianity becomes meaningful and effective when we read closely enough that in our *perscrutatio* we experience an epiphany, or unveiling, of the face of Christ. As we come to know him, we are bound more and more closely in covenant with him. But it is the Holy Spirit who makes Scripture fertile in the heart of the Church, showing us Christ's face and the way to an encounter with him, and giving direction to each of us personally and in our communities. Only then can we obey the Word that has come forth from the words on the biblical page.

When our use of philological, historical, and literary methods of biblical analysis remains open to the Holy Spirit's action, we can read the Bible spiritually and "correctly balance respect for the text's otherness with the fact that it is given to us to live by."[16] Awareness of tradition is an essential part of interpreting the Bible: such an awareness is an *epiclesis*, an invoking of the Spirit upon the biblical "letter" as we follow in the footsteps of many readers throughout history, with their *sensus fidelium* and their unfolding stories of holiness.

Spiritual exegesis is an approach to the Bible in faith, where by faith we mean the belief that in the Bible the Word of God can be found. It is not a technique or method that competes with other methods. Far from it: spiritual exegesis has actually gleaned from other methods a range of valuable insights without which it would be much poorer. As exegesis *in ecclesia*, it seeks to forge a bond between the principle of the Bible's unity, the variety of exegetical and hermeneutical approaches that are available, and the lived narratives of believers. Only this harmony can produce an interpretation that is genuinely of and for the church.

Spiritual exegesis aims to protect the primacy and mystery of the Word contained in Scripture, a Word to which no method can do full justice. When we read spiritually, we acknowledge that methods are necessary, but they are not enough. Their limitations become obvious in cases in which a method ends up using Scripture to justify its own existence, becoming an idol in the process. An introduction to historical-critical methods aptly observes: "Historical-critical methods are as imperfect as all other methods; they do not yield certain or definitive results, nor do they bring forth a text's meaning as if the text had that one meaning alone. Still, they yield one possible meaning among others."[17] Spiritual exegesis as a "global act" is a quest for the deep meaning of a biblical text—a quest so penetrating that when we grasp that meaning, it calls our whole life into question.

> In an ecclesial interpretation of the creative and redeeming Word, a multidimensional exegesis comes into play in which so-called critical or scholarly exegesis ought to be an important dimension, but only one dimension, of the vibrant equilibrium that is faith's universality.[18]

Spiritual reading brings the Bible closer to us, in the conviction that "all of divine Scripture makes up a single book, and this single book is Christ, because all of divine Scripture speaks of Christ and finds its fulfillment in him."[19] The one reason to read spiritually is to come to know Jesus Christ with true Christian *gnosis*—which is dynamic, deeply involving, penetrating, and opens into communion. With the Spirit moving us—since it is the Spirit who interprets Christ's words and silence and guides us toward the fullness of truth (cf. John 16:13)—we can engage in exegesis that is genuinely catholic, universal, *katà tò hólon*. This approach draws the believing reader into the mystery of faith, and into the text that bears witness to that mystery. We will then be moved to make the covenant and dialogue with God that are everywhere in Scripture an important part of our own lives. This is the way toward a living exegesis, toward the living out of our own stories of holiness, and toward the fulfillment of all that Scripture is and can be.

THE BIBLE AS A UNITY

The New Testament authors work with the understanding that all of the Scriptures form a unity. They think in continuity with Scripture, aligning their thoughts with the collection of writings that the Gospels call "the law of Moses, the prophets and the psalms" (Lk. 24:44), or "the law and the prophets" (Matt. 5:17; 7:12). This group of texts did not yet form the defined, closed canon we call the Old Testament or the Hebrew Scriptures.

Let us start with the premise that we will come to understand the past only if we form relationships with the authors we study, to the point of taking on their mindset. If this is the case, we need to take very seriously the New Testament authors' understanding of the unity of the Scriptures. How else will we understand what it means to say that the Easter event happened "according to the Scriptures," unless we enter into the perspective of the Bible as a unity? "Christ died for our sins *in accordance with the scriptures* . . . he was buried, and . . . he was raised on the third day *in accordance with the scriptures*" (1 Cor. 15:3–4 [emphasis mine]). Without the Bible as witness, the Easter event is mute. It is reduced to the puzzling sight of an empty tomb, and Christ is not recognized, but remains the stranger he was to the two disciples on the road to Emmaus. He cannot be proclaimed as the Living one. All that we can do is write up a journalistic account of his career, or a respectful obituary (cf. Lk. 24:19–24).

But if the tomb standing empty after three days (Lk. 24:1–3) is viewed in the light of Scripture and Jesus's words (Lk. 24:6–7), then the Resurrection event can be received in faith ("He is not here, but has risen": Lk. 24:6). Then and then alone, the story of the empty tomb can be announced (Lk. 24:9), preached (Acts 2:22–36), handed down (1 Cor. 15:3), celebrated liturgically by the gathered Christian community (Lk. 24:34), confessed and set down in writing, eventually becoming Scripture in its own right (cf. 1 Cor. 15:3–4). As we may have noticed in the examples just given, the Bible is intrinsically connected to liturgy, and this connection moved the process of formation of the biblical text forward.

In the Psalms, for example, we observe that as the people answer God's word, their prayer becomes an integral part of that Word (C. Westermann). Because of this, the Psalms may be the book of the Bible where the divine-human character of Scripture is easiest to see. The Psalms are also exegetical: they give us clear examples of the phenomena of intrabiblical re-reading (A. Gelin) and rewriting. The final redaction of a given biblical text, its canonical form, conceals stratified reformulations of a base text, which was re-shaped over the course of time: for example, while it was being used in the liturgy, and as it was adapted to times and places different from those in which it was first composed. This process suggests that there is polysemy, a plurality of senses, even at the level of the "letter of the text." One well-known premise of the historical-critical method is that there is a distance between a biblical text and the events of which it speaks, so that the text is already a theological interpretation of the events, "and the literal meaning is already, at least preliminarily, the spiritual meaning" (I. de la Potterie and G. Zevini).

Take, for example, the messianic psalms. Here we have texts that were composed during Israel's monarchy and used during the enthronement ceremony of an anointed king, or *mashiach*. But even after the Babylonian exile and the definitive end of the Jerusalem monarchy, the psalms kept being prayed and sung in the liturgy. This gave them new life, so that instead of commemorating the Messiah of a past era, they came to celebrate the coming, future Messiah. As they were used in the liturgy, they gradually took on an eschatological meaning that was foreign to their climate of origin. This new usage allowed faith and messianic hope to grow in Israel.

When we look at the history of a given biblical text, we see that it is a bearer of multiple semantic possibilities. So the historical meaning of that text is the history of how it took on meaning after meaning during its handing down (*paradosis*), its rereadings (*deuterosis*), and its use in liturgy, up until the time of its placement in the canon. Very much in line with this is the rabbinic and patristic intuition we have already seen in Origen, that a biblical text has multiple senses. In a famous passage of the Talmud, Rabbi Ishmael comments on Jeremiah 23:29, in which the word of God is compared to a hammer that splinters rock. He says, "Just as this hammer makes sparks fly forth, a single passage of scripture yields many meanings," so that "every verse can be read in a variety of ways."[20] The rabbis said elsewhere that "in every word, many lights shine,"[21] and "the Bible has seventy faces."[22] A psalm conveys a similar idea: "One thing God has spoken, two things have I heard: that might belongs to God" (Ps. 62:11) In the writings of the church fathers we hear that "the words of holy Scripture are chiseled stones"[23] whose many facets yield different meanings, so that "from the same words of Scripture . . . several senses can be drawn (*ex eisdem Scripturae verbis . . . plura sentiuntur*). That is, the same words can be understood in different ways (*eadem verba pluribus intellegantur modis*)."[24] Hans Urs von Balthasar has this to say on the subject:

> The four senses of scripture are celebrating a hidden resurrection in today's theology. The *literal sense* appears to be analogous to the *historical-critical* approach, the *spiritual* sense to the *kerygmatic*, the *tropological* to the *existential*, and the *anagogical* to the *eschatological*.[25]

To be involved readers, we need to be aware that the Bible speaks both *about us* and *to us* in our lives today. And we need to live out our response in prayer and action. Reader involvement is integral to the Bible's ecclesial-liturgical character and its ties with tradition, the "living fabric into which all Scripture is woven."[26] The topic of reader response is being studied today in a range of disciplines that are concerned with the act of reading, such as linguistics and reader response criticism. The text is not only a product of certain historical situations; it in turn *produces* history, and can deploy its meaning when it is activated by a community of readers, each of whom welcomes it as addressed to him or her in a very personal way. Without doubt, archaeological and other historical data can tell us something about a biblical passage's author, its intended readers, and its date and place of composition. But the text's historical sense does not end there. The canonical text reaches out in space and time to embrace a circle of new recipients, and in this process the various biblical books are taken away from their human authors and their author is declared to be God by the mediation of the Spirit. This is why we must read the canonical biblical text teleologically as well—that is, looking for its afterlife, what it has brought about over the course of history, its life in tradition. The text doesn't just "have" meaning, it *makes* meaning.

Biblical scholars have begun to take note of the *Wirkungsgeschichte* of biblical texts, as H.-G. Gadamer called the history of their influence.[27] Swiss scholar Ulrich Luz spoke at a conference of the Studiorum Novi Testamenti Societas, in 1990, on "The primacy text (Matt. 16:17–19) in light of its reception history (*Wirkungsgeschichte*)." For Luz, trying to understand the history of a text's impact, how it has been understood and lived out in different historical eras, is a necessary part of any quest for fullness of comprehension. This sort of research takes note of the performative power of texts, which can awaken new ways of understanding them, and it also asks how people live: "The history of a text's effects reveals what we have become through a text over the course of history, and what we might have become."[28]

Luz goes on to ask: How do we decide which truth criteria to apply to the range of interpretations that have emerged over history? How do we know that we are genuinely in contact with a text's meaning? He proposes a criterion of correspondence to the pattern of Jesus's life, as well as a practical *love criterion*: "A new interpretation is true to the extent that it awakens and brings about love"—and love is meant christologically here, as the reality of the risen Lord.[29] This is actually a restatement of a criterion formulated many centuries ago by Augustine, who said that interpretation of the Bible must effectively build up love: "Anyone who thinks that he has understood the divine scriptures or any part of them, but cannot by his understanding build up this double love of God and neighbor, has not yet succeeded in understanding them."[30] We must, Augustine says, keep vigil over Scripture, reading it over and over with focused and loving attention "until its interpretation can be connected with the realm of love."[31] This has always been one of the most basic principles of spiritual reading, and we find it as often in rabbinic as in patristic exegesis. We understand Scripture to the extent to which we live by it.

If our faith allows us to recognize in Scripture the living Word, which pierces until it judges the intentions of the heart (cf. Heb. 4:12), then we will discern in that Word a call that applies to our lives in the here and now. The love criterion of which we just spoke requires that we read those biblical passages that call for love of God and neighbor (cf. Deut. 6:5, Lev. 19:18, Mk. 12:29–31, Matt.

22:37–40, Lk. 10:26–28), and then actually go out and love God and our neighbors. We find a Christological summary of this command in the *mandatum novum* of John 13:34: "Just as I have loved you, you also should love one another."

Lastly, let us recall that exegetical and hermeneutical efforts tend to locate a text's deep truth in its hidden, inner nucleus. We are invited to go "beyond the verse" (E. Levinas) or "beyond the parable" (V. Fusco) to get a sense of the truth of the verse or parable. What is left unsaid in the text is significant.[32] This means that the reader seeking spiritual insight must *inter-legere* (read between the lines), and *intus-legere* (read in depth) to enter into the text's innermost chamber, so to speak, into the intimacy of the divine life hidden in the written words. This is how we can become so drawn into knowing Christ that we are genuinely reborn with him to new life.

SPIRITUAL UNEASE

Because reading Scripture is an ecclesial act, we cannot approach it as a purely technical issue. We need to talk about it in the context of two broader topics: the life of the church, and what it means to be human. We live in a culture subdivided into a tremendous number of specializations, in which the paradigm of *homo technologicus* reigns. Our society is so intent on meeting deadlines and keeping things running smoothly enough to satisfy its own needs that it has turned inward on itself. We forget to breathe deeply and look out into the open, toward distant horizons. So much of what we experience is short-term, and this keeps us tied to externals, to the surface of reality. And so we find ourselves in a condition of spiritual unease and anxiety.

Everywhere we look, obstacles crop up that make our access to Scripture highly problematic. It is hard to experience the Bible as something that generates meaning and hope, that inspires us to take action and that also acts on us, on our lives. These challenges arise in a climate in which we are urged to consume, to be efficient and productive. We are bombarded by visuals and sound. We are asked to buy into myths, such as the myth of spontaneity and of "having it all right away." In our social lives and at work, everything keeps speeding up, and we may find that even our free time has been taken over and scheduled for us.

In the Church we see problems akin to these. There are fractures, hard to heal, between how we pray and how we live, and more broadly between spirituality and life—that is, between what we perceive to be spiritual and what is most human. There are not enough spiritual fathers and mothers among us. Often, church congregations treat their many pastoral and other activities as what is most important. Parish and diocesan life are becoming increasingly bureaucratic, and priests may neglect, sometimes quite noticeably, the critical task of handing down the Christian "gnosis" that comes from knowing God's word (cf. Mal. 2:7). These obstacles may give us the feeling that the Bible is no longer relevant. Or, they may reduce biblical *lectio* to one activity among many. Further, we live in a society in which many people either hardly read at all, or read in a rushed way. We read to distract ourselves, to consume, or to get as much information as we can in as little time as possible. Given habits such as these, we may not feel instantly motivated to read a book as demanding as the Bible, let alone read to discover a presence and enter into relationship with the Other.

And yet a pressing *meaning question* is with us today. We do feel the need to find meaning and direction for our lives. We need guidance in managing the whole personal, relational sphere of our existence. In our competitive society, in which so much is anonymous, impersonal, and individualistic, there is still a longing for a culture of presence. We desire the unification of our fragmented lives, and communion. We look for some sort of unifying reference point that can help us hold our inner selves together when temptations threaten to seduce us and pull us in all directions, away from our center. Society demands that we be productive and efficient, but this expectation is an idol at whose feet the humanness of our lives gets sacrificed. Amidst all of this, we are searching for experiences of gratuity, for a return to *being* as opposed to always *doing*. We may be surrounded by opulence and abundance and we may own many things, yet in this situation we may also feel an urgent desire for radical simplification: to pare ourselves down to the essential, to travel from the outside into the depths, to pass from multiplicity to unity.

In the Church, this means returning to the sources. We need to go to the root of the plant, from which unity can bud again where there has been division and separation. Our return to the sources can open up new spaces and possibilities where there has been suffocating closure. What is essential is to make sure that faith and knowledge of Jesus the Lord really do come first—and that even the ecclesial act of reading Scripture is done in service of this goal, because we are Christians by virtue of the relationships of faith and love that unite us with our Lord (cf. 1 Pet. 1:8). This is why *lectio divina* is an excellent example of a spiritual practice that has flourished since Vatican II, even outside of its traditional monastic setting. It is a practice that allows Christians to reclaim a radical simplicity and forge a bond between prayer and life, between spirituality and what is most basic to being human.

CHAPTER 3

GOD'S WORD AND
HOLY SCRIPTURE

In the first two chapters of this book I offered some reflections in answer to the question, "Why spiritual exegesis"? In the chapters to come, we will ask who should do *lectio divina* and look at how and where it is done. Before we turn to this topic, we need to say something about the Bible's unique status and place in the Church.

SCRIPTURE CONTAINS
THE WORD OF GOD

What is the relationship, exactly, between God's word and the Bible, between Word and Scripture? The Bible itself is witness to the fact that the two realities are not identical. The Word goes beyond the Bible and is not fully captured by it.

God's word is energy, living reality, active and effective (cf. Isa. 55:10–11, Heb. 4:12–13). It is eternal (cf. Ps. 119:89, Isa. 40:8, 1 Pet. 1:25) and all-powerful (cf. Wis. 18:15). God speaks, and the power of his word is made manifest in creation and in history. When God speaks, his word "calls into existence . . . things that do not exist" (Rom. 4:17). This word creates (cf. Gen. 1:3ff, Ps. 33:6–9, Wis. 9:1, Heb. 11:3), and it makes history, which is why the Hebrew *davar* (word) can also mean "history" in the Bible (cf. 1 Kgs. 11:41; 14:19, 29; 15:7, 23, 31; and so throughout). We see that God's word is an entity much more expansive than Scripture. A *davar* is basically a theological reality, an act of revelation from God; it is "God's intervention in the moral and physical evolution of the world."[33] That is, a *davar* is a way in which God says who he is, and it is always coupled with the sending of the divine spirit (*ruach*), since in the Bible "the spirit and the word are two forms of revelation that are always contemporaneous."[34] God's word is an act of self-giving that becomes presence in dialogue, a reaching out toward meeting us in *berit* (covenant).

The New Testament says that in these last days, "God has spoken to us by a Son" (Heb. 1:2). The Father's only-begotten is God's definitive Word. As the Logos, he was in the beginning with God, *was* God, presided over the creation of the world (cf. John 1:1ff), became flesh (John 1:14), and was born of a woman (Gal. 4:4) by the power of the Holy Spirit (cf. Lk. 1:35). In the New Testament economy, God's word becomes the person of the Son himself, who tells the Father's story and opens a pathway for believers to communion with the God whom no one has ever seen (John 1:18). It should be clear by now that the Bible is not God's word in a direct sense, and so it is not precisely correct to call it God's word.

On this subject, there is a critical passage in the Vatican II document *Dei Verbum* that went through a number of revisions before a final draft was agreed upon. The *textus prior* stated:

> The sacred Scriptures not only contain the word of God, but are truly the word of God.

In the *textus emendatus*, this passage was retouched and the words "not only" (*non tantum*) were omitted, so that the result was:

> The sacred Scriptures contain the word of God and are truly the word of God.

The council fathers were still unsatisfied with this revision, and rightly so. They kept reworking the text, eventually adding a crucial expression that is found in both the *textus denuo emendatus* and in the *textus adprobatus*:

> The sacred Scriptures contain the word of God, and because they are inspired (*quia inspiratae*), they are truly the word of God *(verbum Dei)*.

We may place this statement alongside a similar one in *Dei Verbum* 9 (which is absent from the *textus prior*):

> Sacred scripture is the utterance of God (*locutio Dei*) put down as it is in writing under the inspiration of the Holy Spirit.[35]

Scripture is *verbum Dei* or *locutio Dei* in that it is divinely inspired. The way in which the conciliar documents evolved suggests that the council fathers wanted to avoid stating that the Bible is directly and immediately God's word. The word of God transcends Scripture, and since the biblical authors were human and only human, we should say that "the word of God is contained in the Bible," and that the Bible is God's word only because of the Holy Spirit. As in Origen's allegorical interpretation of the Gospel episode in which Jesus enters Jerusalem riding a donkey and a colt, we can say that "the scriptures, Old and New Testament, transport the Logos of God,"[36] God's word. Or in the words of another early Christian theologian, Gaudentius of Brescia: "The whole corpus of divine Scripture, both the Old and New Testaments, contain the Son of God."[37]

In Jewish tradition, Scripture is a "mouthpiece." It is "the interpreter of an original word that cannot be interpreted," and is "the witness to a process in which the infinite word, the *davar*, shrunk itself to fit within the letters on the page, but without becoming totally synonymous with the signs that capture it."[38] The written Torah is now normative, a definitive collection. To open it (the Hebrew verb is *patach*) to understanding, we need to pore over it and ask it questions (*darash*) as we work tirelessly to interpret it. There is a story in the Talmud that suggests that the Torah itself asks to be interpreted. If all the words in the Torah are added up, those that are found to fall in its exact center are the double verb *darosh darash* ("he inquired with care") in Leviticus 10:16. The root of this verb is also the source of the term *midrash*.

> The early sages were called *soferim* because they counted (from the verb *safar*) every letter of Torah. They said that . . . the expression *darosh darash* (Lev 10:16) marks the exact middle of the words of Torah.[39]

In an analogous way, Scripture in the Christian economy is a witness to God's word, but it does not coincide with it. Jesus Christ the Son, God's eternal Word, is not contained in human language and cannot be circumscribed within it. Even the four Gospels, filled as they are with different human words and perspectives, only come close to the eternal word but do not express it conclusively. Since the Word cannot be identified with Scripture, being infinitely vaster than everything that is in the Bible, it can be heard and understood only with the help of the Spirit's interpretation. The Spirit must explain what has been set down in Scripture regarding the Son and the Father. Jesus himself did not write anything, and the New Testament is already an interpretation, a witness to the Messiah who interpreted Torah by fulfilling it. The New Testament is also a re-reading of the Scriptures (the Old Testament in this case) in light of faith in the risen Christ. It is a witness to Jesus's life and ministry, death and resurrection in the light of Scripture.

Just as the Word comes before Scripture and goes beyond it, it is also true that in a sense Scripture precedes the Word. Because of this, there is a *perichoresis* or circular movement between Word and Scripture: "The Word that has taken place becomes Scripture so that it can go back to being Word with Scripture's help, and there find its fulfillment as a Word interpreting Scripture."[40]

The Christian understanding throughout history has been that "*Christus in littera continetur*":[41] and so "Scripture as a whole is a great 'sacrament' which contains, in a sort of material husk, the mystery of salvation whose center is Christ. Guided by the Spirit, I must enter through the 'letter' and keep going into the depths of mystery, where I meet him."[42] The traditional understanding of Scripture has always found the analogy of the Incarnation helpful in this regard.

THE INCARNATION ANALOGY

For the Christian reader, Scripture is the body of Christ: "His body is the ceaseless handing down of Scripture."[43] Traditionally, the body of Scripture has been considered, by analogy with Christ's physical body, to be a form of embodiment (*ensomátosis*) of the Logos.

In the Creed, the Word's becoming flesh in the virgin Mary (*et incarnatus est de Spiritu Sancto ex Maria Virgine*) closely parallels the embodiment of God's word in the word of the prophets (*credo in Spiritum Sanctum . . . qui locutus est per prophetas*). Both events are overseen by the Holy Spirit.

Just as there is a *kenosis* in which the Word descends into flesh (*sarx*), there is also a *kenosis* in which the Word lowers himself into written human words (*graphé*). This incarnation analogy, which we find again and again in the church fathers, also appears in the *Dei Verbum*:

> . . . in sacred scripture, without prejudice to God's truth and holiness, the marvelous 'condescension' of eternal wisdom is plain to be seen, 'that we may come to know the ineffable loving-kindness of God and see for ourselves the thought and care he has given to accommodating his language to our nature.' Indeed the words

of God, expressed in human language, are in every
way like human speech, just as the Word of the eternal Father, when he took on himself the weak flesh of
human beings, became like them. (*Dei Verbum* 13)

The *Dei Verbum* uses the biblical and patristic theme of God's
"condescension" (*synkatábasis*) to explain God's bending down,
as it were, to reach men and women in the various situations in
which they find themselves. "Condescension" is the act of mercy
with which God comes to dwell among humans. This act is
revealed both when God's word becomes flesh, and when that
word becomes Scripture. God's condescension allowed the Word
to be made present in written texts that are exposed to the risks
involved in redaction and transmission. Likewise, God presided
over the Incarnation, even though this led to the Word's death
on the cross. None of these events have compromised God's truth
and holiness.

If the Word became flesh, similar to humans in all things except
for sin (Heb. 4:15), then God's word also entered into human
language in Scripture without becoming falsehood or sin. Rather,
God's truth and holiness remain.

This is the "scandal" of the Incarnation and of the Bible. Just as
we are called to recognize the Messiah in Jesus of Nazareth (cf.
Mk. 8:29), the Son of God in a crucified criminal (cf. Mk. 15:39),
the Holy One in a man who was made sin (cf. 2 Cor. 5:21), the
Righteous One in someone counted among evildoers (cf. Lk.
22:37), and God's Presence in the godless place of crucifixion,[44]
so we are also called to discern God's word in human scripture.

The one Word is there to be found in a vast collection of biblical books with their expressive diversity and their tensions, even contradictions, in content and theological perspective. We are called to recognize that the Spirit is active in the historical processes by which the biblical text has come into being: oral tradition, written recension, rereading and rewriting, textual corruptions, scribal glosses and revisions during the text's transmission. If we can accept the mystery of the incarnation, we can also accept the mystery of God's word in the Bible, and vice versa. But this is a Spirit-guided process that takes place in faith.

We need to accept God's word in its incomplete, human expression, just as we are to accept the Son's divine quality in Jesus's fragile human body. It was, once again, Origen who helped make this analogy between Scripture and incarnation popular among subsequent patristic writers. In the West, Augustine wrote memorably of how the fullness of God's revelation happened in a *kenosis* visible in the humility of letters and flesh:

> There is but one single utterance of God amplified throughout all the scriptures, dearly beloved. Through the mouths of many holy persons a single Word makes itself heard, that Word who, being God-with-God in the beginning, has no syllables, because he is not confined by time. Yet we should not find it surprising that to meet our weakness he descended to the discrete sounds we use, for he also descended to take to himself the weakness of our human body.[45]

In the East, Maximus the Confessor followed Origen's lead:

> The Logos of God is called flesh not only inasmuch as He became incarnate, but in another sense as well. When He [who] is contemplated in his true simplicity, in His principial state with God the Father (cf. John 1:1–2) (. . .) draws near to men (. . .) He selects things which are familiar to them, combining together various stories, symbols, parables, and dark sayings; and in this way He becomes flesh. Thus at the first encounter our intellect comes into contact not with the naked Logos but with the incarnate Logos, that is, with various sayings and stories. The incarnate Logos, though Logos by nature, is flesh in appearance. Hence most people think they see flesh and not the Logos, although in fact He is the Logos. The intellect—that is, the inner meaning—of Scripture is other than what it seems to most people. For the Logos becomes flesh in each of the recorded sayings.[46]

The Incarnation happened so as to foster encounter, communion, dialogue, and covenant between God and people, and Scripture exists for the same purpose: "The Word has always become flesh in the Scriptures so as to pitch his tent among us," Origen said,[47] applying to the Bible what the prologue of the Fourth Gospel says about the Incarnation (cf. John 1:14). In the Bible, Christ is contained as *Verbum abbreviatum*,[48] the one Word of God who was already present in the Old Testament as *Verbum incarnandum*, and who condenses and summarizes in himself the many words with which God had been progressively revealed.

The Bible, then, is a mediator of the one Word of God. Like the Eucharist, it "contains the Lord as Word and as Spirit,"[49] and like the Eucharist, it communicates Christ to those who are led by the Spirit to receive it in faith.

WORD AND EUCHARIST

The Word-Eucharist parallelism we have been considering was a major theme of the Second Vatican Council, and can be found in many of its documents.[50] The Constitution on the Liturgy (*Sacrosanctum Concilium* 56) states:

> . . . the liturgy of the word and the eucharistic liturgy are so closely connected with each other that they form but one single act of worship.

The Church expresses its essence in the liturgy, where Scripture and bread are metabolized into Christ's body and blood. There is an intrinsic unity between Word and sacrament: they include each other, and in their *perichoresis* they are an epiphany in the present moment of the fullness of the salvation event brought about in the Lord Jesus Christ.

The *Dei Verbum* states:

> The church has always venerated the divine scriptures as *(sicut et)* it has venerated the Body of the Lord, in

> that it never ceases, above all in the sacred liturgy, to
> partake of the bread of life and to offer it to the faithful
> from the one table of the word of God and the Body of
> Christ. (DV 21)

Unfortunately, the definitive version of this text weakened the parallelism between Scripture and body of Christ by replacing the word "velut" in the *textus denuo emendatus* with "sicut et," because some conciliar fathers were reluctant to see the table of the Word too closely assimilated (*nimis assimilare*) with that of the Eucharist.

The transition from "velut" in the earlier draft to "sicut et" underscores the different ways in which the Church venerates Scripture and Christ's body. Needless to say, *Dei Verbum* and other Vatican II documents reflect debates on issues that were controversial at the time, and that had to be resolved via compromise during the Council's deliberations. Yet these writings have also pointed us toward a path on which we must continue to walk to activate the Council's spirit. As we have seen, the close bond between Word and Eucharist has its roots in the Bible itself, and is spoken of by church fathers going back as far as Ignatius of Antioch. The same connection is made by the medieval Cistercian and Victorine authors. From at least Origen's time, Christians used the same symbolic and theological language to speak of the Incarnation, the Scriptures, and the Eucharist. In the sixth chapter of John's Gospel, Christ calls himself "bread of life" in a double sense: because he is the Logos, God's word who reveals the Father, and because he is Eucharistic food and drink. Ignatius of Antioch says that he takes refuge "in the Gospel as in the flesh of Jesus,"[51] and Jerome writes:

> Since the flesh of the Lord is true food and his blood is true drink, in the anagogical sense, the only good in the present world is this: to feed on his flesh and blood not only in the mystery of the altar, but also in reading the Scriptures. For true food and drink is what is received from God's word, that is, knowledge of the Scriptures.[52]

Through the writings of Christians like Jerome, it gradually became traditional to say that Jesus broke bread, and broke open the Scriptures. Scripture, it was said, could be "chewed" as if it were bread, and there are biblical precedents for this idea (Ezekiel eats a scroll that God gives him—Ezek. 2:8–3:3—and the seer John also consumes a small scroll taken from an angel's hand in Rev. 10:8–11.) It also became traditional to compare how the Word was conceived by the Holy Spirit in Mary and took on flesh in her, with the Word's conception in every believer by the Holy Spirit during *lectio divina*.

The church fathers were well aware that reading the Bible is an encounter and an entry to communion with God, as is the sacrament of the Eucharist. Jerome wrote: "Are you praying? You are speaking with the Bridegroom. Are you reading? He is speaking to you."[53] For Ambrose of Milan, "We speak with God when we pray; we hear him when we read the writings that are inspired by God."[54]

Let us go back over what we have said. When we read the Bible in the Holy Spirit, aware of its unity in Christ, and when in faith we take it into our hearts within a church community, it can become powerfully nourishing for us: food given by God, "bread of life." The Bible often speaks of God's word as spiritual food for which people hunger and thirst.[55] Such passages inspired a patristic tradition that continued to develop this theme by showing the connection between the nourishment of the Word and the food of the Eucharist. Church fathers eventually began to speak of two tables: the table of the Word, and that of the Eucharistic bread and wine.

This tradition tells us that the believer needs the food of God's word in order to live: "Those who do not nourish themselves with God's word do not live."[56] God's word is not neutral, but accomplishes things and brings judgment with itself: "God's word is our manna, and when the divine word comes to us, it brings salvation to some and chastisement to others."[57]

The Bible has, as we have seen, a sacramental quality in that it can place us in contact with Christ, who speaks through it:

> The one who understands the meaning of an apostolic writing perfectly, without distorting it, receives—just as the apostle did—the Messiah who speaks and lives with the apostle, and that person also possesses Christ's teaching.[58]

For the medieval theologian Rupert of Deutz,

> All of Scripture is God's one word. . . . When we read holy Scripture, we touch the word of God and have God's Son before our eyes "in a mirror, in an enigma" (cf. 1 Cor. 13:12).[59]

The medieval author of *De unitate Ecclesiae conservanda* is very concise: "By body of Christ, we mean God's Scripture as well."[60]

Scripture and Eucharist are therefore both Christ's sacramental body, and the words of the Eucharistic institution can be understood as referring aptly enough also to the scriptural word. Origen writes:

> It was not the visible bread he held in his hands that the Word God called his body; rather, it was the Word in whose mystery that bread was to be broken. And it was not the visible drink that he called his blood, but the Word in whose mystery that drink was to be poured out.[61]

Jerome followed Origen:

> I consider the Gospel to be like Jesus' body. . . . And when he says, "the one who eats my flesh" . . . although this can be understood also of the sacrament, the body and blood of Christ in a truer sense are the word of the Scriptures.[62]

This is not a denial of the reality of the Eucharistic body, which Origen calls "typical and symbolic,"[63] but is a way of saying that the body received in the Eucharist is symbolic in relationship to the Logos himself, whose body and blood, in a deep and true sense, are Scripture.[64]

Flesh and blood of God's word, Scripture is food and drink meant to satisfy all of humanity.[65] To take up the Bible is to eat and drink Christ who is present in it:

> Drink from both chalices, the Old and New Testament, because in both you drink Christ (*quia in utroque Christum bibis*). . . . Divine Scripture is swallowed and consumed. . . . *One does not live by bread alone, but by every word of God* (cf. Lk. 4:4).[66]

The Eucharistic liturgy commemorates the way Jesus gathered all of Scripture into his hands, just as he did with the Eucharistic bread, and offered it to believers as their sustenance. Rupert of Deutz, in his commentary on John, wrote rather audaciously:

> [Jesus] took the book . . . and opened it, that is, he received from God's power all of holy Scripture so as to fulfill it in himself . . . the Lord Jesus therefore took the bread of the Scriptures in his hands when, incarnate according to the Scriptures, he endured the passion and rose again. He took bread in his hands and gave thanks when, fulfilling the Scriptures, he offered himself to the Father as a sacrifice of grace and truth.[67]

The Eastern and Western churches have always venerated Scripture in their liturgical traditions as they do the living Lord, recognizing his presence in the Bible as in the Eucharistic bread and wine. Scripture and Eucharist are intrinsically related and are in *perichoresis*. Both presences are founded uniquely on God's self-giving, his sending of the Word, which takes place through the Holy Spirit. This is why the *epiclesis*, or invoking of the Spirit, is essential to each celebration of the Word (which has its own legitimacy, dignity, and efficacy even apart from the Eucharistic liturgy, because of Scripture's sacramental quality) and to each Eucharistic celebration. Scripture has ecclesial status and can rightly be called a sacrament.

SCRIPTURE IS A SACRAMENT

"Such is the force and power of the word of God that it . . . is a pure and unfailing fount of spiritual life" (*Dei Verbum* 21). In the liturgy, Christ "is present in his word since it is he himself who speaks when the holy scriptures are read in church" (*Sacrosanctum Concilium* 7). Through the Bible, "God speaks to his people, Christ is still proclaiming his gospel" (ibid., 33). The Council stressed that the Word powerfully expresses God's covenant, is a gift offered to God's holy people, and is a place of divine presence.

Sadly, a separation between sacrament and Word has persisted into the post-conciliar years and decades, along with the notion that the sacrament gives grace while the biblical word gives doctrine, or that the sacrament is effective, whereas the word can only teach and prepare people to receive the sacrament. But unless God's word is experienced within the sacramental economy to the point of being received as a sacrament that confers power and grace—and not merely as a communication of truth, precept, and doctrine—it will be no more than a word *about* God and a prelude to the Eucharistic celebration.[68]

We need to be clear on this: there is *one* presence of Christ in God's word and in the Eucharist. Christ gave his life proclaiming the Word and explaining Scripture, and he explained Scripture and revealed the Word by offering his body and blood. This makes the Eucharist both a gesture and a proclamation (cf. 1 Cor. 11:26), and the effective word, as it is fulfilled, is also both proclamation and gesture. "The pattern of this revelation unfolds through deeds and words which are intrinsically connected: the works performed by God in the history of salvation show forth and confirm the doctrine and realities signified by the words; the words, for their part, proclaim the works, and bring to light the mystery they contain" (*Dei Verbum* 2). Revelation is not only *locutio Dei*, because *dicere Dei est facere* and *facere Dei est dicere*.

In this pattern of revelation, God "from the fullness of his love, addresses men and women as his friends (cf. Ex. 33:11, John 15:14–15), and lives among them (cf. Bar. 3:38) in order to invite and receive them into his own company" (*Dei Verbum* 2). Christ is the primordial sacrament of God's revelation, in Origen's words, because he is the one mediator between God and human beings (cf. 1 Tim. 2:5). But there are other sacraments of revelation. There is the Church, "at once manifesting and actualizing the mystery of God's love for humanity" (*Gaudium et Spes* 45). There is the Eucharist, an epiphany of the love with which Christ loved humanity to the end; and there is Scripture, which communicates God's word and in which "the Father who is in heaven comes lovingly to meet his children and talks with them" (*Dei Verbum* 21). Each in its own way, Scripture, Eucharist, and the Church are all Christ's "body." They shed light on each other mutually and interpret one another. This tells us that the act of reading the biblical text has an intrinsic relationship to the church community, and should always have the Eucharist as its *télos* or fulfillment.

Scripture, with its sacramental divine-human quality, is a *signum* or sign: a material thing that holds and reveals Christ's mystery and allows us to engage with God in a personal way. We listen and God speaks, revealing the mystery of who he is in the face of Christ. New possibilities for love and communion open. We go from listening to knowing to loving, as Israel is asked to do in the *Shema*: "Hear, O Israel: the Lord is our God, the Lord alone. You shall love the Lord your God . . ." (Deut. 6:4–5, Mk. 12:29). As Christ in his incarnation was *sacramentum Dei*, so Scripture in the course of revelation is *sacramentum Dei*. It prolongs the Christ event and Christ's action in the Church just as all the other sacraments do. Gregory the Great, viewing Scripture and Christ as intrinsically related and finding the real presence of the Redeemer's saving work in the Scriptures, says that they hold "the incarnation, passion, death, and resurrection of the Lord."[69] In the words of a modern scholar, "Gregory describes the Scripture-Christ relationship in sacramental terms. Scripture does more than signify Christ's mystery in advance; it is also an initial actualization of it."[70]

If we say the Bible is a book—which is like saying that the Eucharist is bread and wine—we need to add that it too is a sacrament, a place where grace is poured out, a means of communion with God, a revelation of the divine presence. Unless we approach this book in faith, as a true sign of the communication that is ongoing between God and humans, it will not yield grace or communion. When we have faith, and only then, does the Bible release "the gospel . . . the power of God for salvation to everyone who has faith . . . it in the righteousness of God is revealed through faith for faith; as it is written, 'The one is righteous will live by faith'" (Rom. 1:16–17).

The Bible is sacramental even in its structure. It has an outer and an inner aspect. Believers, led by the Spirit who acts to reveal God, must pass from the outer aspect or level of meaning to the inner one. There are a number of patristic expressions for this: we go from letter to spirit, we peel back the husk to get to the kernel, we look for the fruit amidst the leaves. We are not to allegorize inappropriately and produce some "other" meaning. What we are doing is delving into the text's own depth, its potential for communion. In this depth we find Christ, who is the unity and fulfillment of all Scripture and wants to be in a covenant relationship with us. We should rest in Scripture as the beloved disciple rested his head on Jesus's heart, since "what is meant by 'heart of Christ' is sacred Scripture, which reveals Christ's heart."[71] Let us remember that the Bible is historical, theological, and liturgical at the same time: it witnesses to historical events that are theologically interpreted in the light of faith, and that take on new life in the liturgical celebration.

The Bible's sacramental structure cannot be separated from that of the Eucharist. This was the main point of an address given on October 5, 1964, by the Melkite bishop Msgr. Neophytos Edelby, titular archbishop of Edessa and patriarchal counselor, during the Second Vatican Council's third session. At that time, the second part of the *schema* on divine revelation was being discussed. Msgr. Edelby began by saying that "the first theological principle of any interpretation of sacred Scripture" is that "the sending of the Holy

Spirit cannot be separated from the sending of the incarnate Word," and that "the aim of Christian exegesis is to understand Scripture in light of the risen Christ." He continued forcefully: "Scripture is a liturgical and prophetic reality. It is a proclamation (*kerygma*) before it is a book; it is the Holy Spirit's testimony of the coming of Christ, whose most powerful moment is the Eucharistic liturgy." Msgr. Edelby went on to say that "in the post-Tridentine controversy, Scripture was viewed as a written norm first and foremost," but we are to consider the Bible "the consecration of salvation history under the species of the human word, which cannot be separated from the Eucharistic consecration, during which all of history is summed up in the body of Christ." The relationship with tradition comes in here: "This consecration requires an *epiclesis*, and the *epiclesis* is salutary tradition. Tradition is the epiclesis of salvation history, the theophany of the Holy Spirit, without which history cannot be understood and Scripture is dead letters."

Scripture must therefore be interpreted "within salvation history as a whole."[72] When it is proclaimed in the liturgy, and above all in the Eucharistic celebration, it has the powerful effect of making it possible for us to experience Christ's presence and communion with him. But in our personal *lectio divina*—and even more so if we practice *lectio divina* as a community—we can also experience real communion with Christ. When, through Scripture, we listen to and receive God's word in faith, we hear it as addressed to us in the most personal way possible. Even more than that, we see, hear, and touch the Word of life (cf. 1 John 1:1). Scripture always speaks simultaneously to all people and to each of us individually. Whenever the scriptural word speaks to the plural "you" of the gathered community, it does so by challenging each singular "you." And when a biblical passage is addressed to an individual, it has his or her community affiliation in mind. The Word is spoken to individuals who cannot be separated from the communities in which they live.

CHAPTER 4

THE WHOLE BIBLE
AS A UNITY

The attitude of "hearing the word of God reverently" (*Dei Verbum* 1), which we express by interpreting Scripture "with its divine authorship in mind," also involves paying attention to the "unity of the whole of scripture" (*DV* 12). Only the unity of the Bible, on which its use in the liturgy is based, allows us to make sense of and defend its sacramental aspect and receive it as revelatory, inspiring, and an incarnation of the Word. *Listening*, we have said, is the gateway to interpreting the Bible spiritually within the church community. And the Bible to which we listen is the one that has been passed on to us as the canonical text.

THE CANON

The history of the formation of the biblical canon is a very complex one that we cannot explore in depth here. One key point is that the canon's closure consisted, in substance, in the decision to ratify a practice that was already well established in both Jewish and Christian circles. Books were recognized as canonical because they had been read regularly in Jewish and Christian liturgical assemblies. Canonization was a response to what had already become tradition, and it was an ecclesial-liturgical process: books entered the canon because they kept people in dialogue with their God. A book that could do this clearly contained God's word and was able to help people live in God's covenant and presence.

A canon establishes mutual belonging between a community and its scripture. According to Nehemiah (ch. 8), the Torah became "canonical" when a collection of legal and narrative texts that were already seen as authoritative were proclaimed in a liturgical setting, in such a way that all of the people who had gathered together could understand. Many of them wept when they heard the Word (Neh. 8:9). This vignette from Israel's history shows how canonization is "the juncture of 'Scripture' and biblical 'reading': in the crucible of canon, Scripture is found to be consecrated in its role of *miqra* ('recitation' or 'reading')."[73]

In a study of the Song of Songs, a text whose canonicity was long debated and challenged in the ancient world, Anne-Marie Pelletier proposes an intriguing hypothesis. From what we know of how the Song was traditionally recited and used, the goal was not so much to "explain" the text as it was to make the reader (or hearer) a participant in the book's two-voice dialogue. Pelletier suggests that it is precisely this dialogue form that makes the Song a revelatory text and justifies its entry into the canon. Placed as it is in the center of the Bible, the Song of Songs can then be seen as a concentrated form of the love dialogue that pervades all of Scripture, and in which canonical Scripture wishes to involve readers. This makes the Song of Songs a sort of "interior duplicate" of the whole Bible, a text that reflects in itself, in miniature, the biblical macrotext. The "spiritual needs"[74] that led to the Song of Song's being canonized are therefore the same needs to which the Song, and all of canonical Scripture, continue to respond as they invite hearers to take part in a dialogue between an "I" and a "you", a love relationship and the covenant's demanding grace. For "the canon's authority resides in the life-giving dialogue that the community has with it."[75] And so the many books (*tà biblía*) enclosed in the canon open into the one Book whose unity testifies to both the diachronic and synchronic unity of the believing people, and to the oneness of God who is the Book's "author" (*Dei Verbum* 11).

REDACTION

Alongside the canonical unity of *Scriptura tota*, we need to remember that when we read Scripture and hear the Word, we are in contact with the final redaction of the biblical text. Both a text's final redaction and the canon itself have hermeneutical value: it is through them that we reach the message, the word of God. Studying a text's successive redactions and the different traditions at play in it show us the path that revelation has taken, and how the Spirit has been active over time and in history. But it is by way of the text's final redaction that God speaks to us today, not by means of hypothetical, reconstructed original texts. Regarding the formation of the Pentateuch, the so-called "new criticism" calls for attention to the final redaction of texts, rather than to their origins and the hypothetical "documents" or sources that shaped them. During the compositional process through which the Old Testament was formed, multiple rereadings emerged over time of events such as the Exodus, presenting different theological perspectives. In some cases, theologically distant narratives of the same event were placed side by side, as in the first two chapters of Genesis, where there are two creation accounts. Laws were preserved that give different instructions on the same topics, and in the single book of the Psalms, certain relatively late theological developments (such as the belief that humans have eternal life in communion with God; see Ps. 49) are found along with the more ancient belief that death ends human existence, with no prospect of eternity. These examples show that the Bible is a composite unity. We can rediscover the unity of the Pentateuch even as we take account of the various legal codes and theologies found in it. We can also observe the redactional unity of the book of Isaiah, even though we know that the parts of the book attributed to Second and Third Isaiah are re-readings, applications of the oracles of the prophet Isaiah (who lived in the eighth century BCE) to a later cultural context. So if "it was through the *prophet* that God spoke to the people of Jerusalem, it is through the *book* of Isaiah that God speaks to us today."[76]

SCRIPTURA SUI IPSIUS INTERPRES

Only the unity of Scripture allows us to activate the principle whereby Scripture interprets itself. This is not to say that we should ignore the fact that many biblical texts and institutions (such as ancient Israel's monarchy) were heavily indebted to the literatures and cultures of neighboring peoples. In fact, we need to study the extra-biblical world if we wish to explain the Bible adequately. The Bible's unity does mean that the biblical context (Old and New

Testament) gives a radically new meaning and orientation to what was borrowed from elsewhere.

It is known that there is a relationship between a section of the book of Proverbs (22:17–23, 12) and the ancient Egyptian text *Instructions of Amenemope*. To give another example, in Philippians 4:8, Paul encourages the Christians of Philippi to follow several moral ideals that are also known to us from Stoic ethics. But Proverbs uses *Amenemope's* wisdom teaching to teach faith in YHWH (cf. Prov. 22:19), and the book presents Egyptian ethical instruction in such a way as to shed light on the actions of YHWH *go'el*, the redeemer (cf. Prov. 22:22–23). In Philippians, Paul urges Christians to take to heart (*phronein*) several virtues that were typical of Stoic philosophy, but he subordinates this advice to the commands to "stand firm in the Lord" (Phil. 4:1), to "let the same mind be in you (*phronein*) as was in Christ Jesus" (cf. Phil. 2:5), and to "keep on doing the things that you have learned and received and heard and seen in me" (cf. Phil. 4:9). Paul's language in the first few chapters of 1 Corinthians shows that there is an inevitable clash between human forms of knowledge and the gospel, the heart of which can never be other than the "message about the cross" (1 Cor. 1:18). This message about the cross is not consistent at all with the world's thinking, but calls it radically into question.

Scriptura sui ipsius interpres means that within the Bible there is a basic principle: faith in the one God YHWH who, by freeing Israel from slavery, revealed himself in history as a personal God to invite Israel into a covenant relationship: "I am YHWH your God." This principle confers unity upon the many, diverse texts in the Bible, and gives what is borrowed from other cultures a new orientation.

In the New Testament, the unifying hermeneutical principle is faith in Jesus Christ who died and rose, and who is the definitive revelation of the God of Abraham, Isaac, and Jacob, and the mediator of the new covenant (cf. Heb. 7:22, 8:6, 9:15). The faith that brought the biblical texts into being still enlivens them and makes them revelatory, and not simply ethical or edifying. And faith takes us, when we read, to a place where we meet and experience the one God.

TYPOLOGY

Intrabiblical rereadings give us many examples of how Scripture reads "itself." The exodus event, for one, is woven throughout the Bible via numerous reinterpretations, and we can even list various types of approaches that were used to make the event current for a later generation. The cultural approach (cf. Exod. 12:1–13, 16 ff.), the prophetic-typological approach (Amos, Hosea, Jeremiah, Second Isaiah), and the midrashic approach (cf. Wis. 10:15–22, 27 and 16:1–19, 22), are several of these.

Typology came to play an important role in thinking about the relationship between the Old and New Testaments, since it was used by the New Testament writers themselves. It is important for a spiritual understanding of the Bible, but is highly controversial today and calls for careful discernment. As Origen tells us, a relationship of typological correspondence between an Old Testament situation and a New Testament one does not annul the historical significance of what came first—it actually depends on its historicity. Commenting on a passage of the Letter to the Galatians

(4:21–24), Origen writes, "What then shall we say? That Isaac was not born in the flesh? That Sarah did not give birth to him? That he was not circumcised? . . . What is marvelous (is that) . . . he gives allegorical significance to events that undoubtedly did happen according to the flesh."[77] In another place, Origen writes, "And in the passage where the Apostle says, 'Abraham had two sons . . .', who doubts that these things are to be taken literally? . . . But the Apostle adds, 'These are allegories.'"[78]

Typology also confirms the permanent prophetic value of the "type" event: this is exactly what we learn from the many and varied interpretations of the Exodus that flowered in ancient Israel over the course of centuries. As regards the relationship between Old and New Testament, we might pursue a three-phase rather than a two-phase typological approach, inspired (of course) by Origen, who speaks of shadow, image, and truth. In this perspective, both type and antitype remain open to an eschatological fulfillment that still lies ahead as much for Christians as for Jews. The fulfillment in Christ confessed by Christians is an "already" that opens into a "not yet." It does not take anything away from Israel's hope, nor does it flatten the historical richness and prophetic potency of Israel's Scriptures. When typology opens into eschatology, it actually does best what it is able to do, which is highlight the continuity of God's revealing action throughout history, up until its eschatological fulfillment.

THE CHRISTOLOGICAL UNITY OF THE SCRIPTURES

We receive from the Bible itself a unifying and unquestionably central hermeneutical principle: the Passover mystery.

The Passover event in the Old Testament appears as fulfilled prophecy in the New Testament Easter event. The Bible can be read in the light of this unifying principle. When it is read in this way, it becomes a narrative synthesis of a single theological mystery that spans the vision of the Lamb slain "from the foundation of the world" (Rev. 13:8) to the eschatological coming of the "Lamb standing as if it had been slaughtered" (Rev. 5:6).

The implication of this is that all of the Scriptures have Christ at their center: the unity of the Bible is unity in Christ. There is widespread agreement on this in Christian tradition. Christ is both "the Lord of the prophets"[79] and the one who fulfills prophecy, the one "on whose account and for whom every prophecy exists."[80] It is Christ who, "by rising and ascending to heaven, opened the book."[81] He is the Word and its interpretation, and he alone is capable of explaining Scripture, because "he created the words of the holy Testaments and he himself revealed their meaning to us."[82]

It is often said in Christian tradition that Moses wrote about Christ (cf. John 5:46), and that the Torah of Moses, the prophets and the psalms speak about him (cf. Lk. 24:44). Christ opens people's minds to understand the Scriptures (cf. Lk. 24:45), and in explaining them he reveals himself. In the last chapter of Luke, the episode of the two disciples walking to Emmaus forms an inclusion with the episode early in the Gospel in which Jesus's parents find him at the Temple "after three days" (Lk. 2:46), talking with the teachers and surprising them with his understanding of the Scriptures. Three days after his death, the two disciples of Emmaus encounter him living as he explains the Scriptures (cf. Lk. 24:27). This is where we meet the risen Christ: where Scripture is being explained. And the Bible can be understood when Christ is seen as its hermeneutical focal point, at which moment the transition can be made from non-faith (cf. Lk. 24:41) to faith and praise of God (cf. Lk. 24:53). Exegesis done in faith opens of its own accord into prayer: exegesis and theology, understanding of Scripture and prayer are all brought together in the mystery of faith. When Ignatius of Antioch's opponents tried to divide the Old from the New Testament, he insisted that Christ holds all of Scripture's contents together in a seamless whole: ". . . my archives are Jesus Christ. . . . My authentic archives are his cross, and death, and resurrection, and the faith which bears on these things."[83]

The apostles, in their preaching, developed the relationship between ancient Scripture and the Christ event in such a way that we cannot speak of a simple succession. It is mutual illumination, as the Easter event is interpreted in light of Scripture and also *interprets* Scripture. This makes it "the hermeneutical key that allows us to understand the scriptures that had been proclaimed, but without the illumination of Scripture the Easter experience would remain an enigma" (J. Dupont). The Christian tradition of reading Scripture sees the two Testaments as interdependent, with Christ as the cornerstone of both: "Christ is found in both Testaments because Christ himself is their *consensus*."[84] For the patristic authors, the testaments are intrinsically bound together: "The Old Testament is revealed in the New (*revelatum*), and . . . the New Testament is veiled in the Old (*velatum*)."[85] In Christ, the veil that remains in the Jewish reading of the Old Testament is removed (cf. 2 Cor. 3:14).

Christ is the one who "fulfills" Scripture (cf. John 19:28), and when we read that what was written about him in the Law, the prophets, and the Psalms (cf. Lk. 24:44) has been fulfilled, we are not meant to take this according to the letter. What is meant is that God's will, revealed in Scripture, has been grasped and carried out. This is why we find the word *dei* ("it is necessary") repeated three times in chapter 24 of Luke (vv. 7, 26, and 44). It refers to divine necessity, and is related here to Jesus's passion, death, and resurrection as the doxological fulfillment of "everything that is written" (cf. Lk. 18:31–33). The Scriptures' fulfillment in Christ is a revelation event that gives new order to what was revealed in the past. As a result, the movement of revelation is not in one direction only, but is an exchange in which Christological fulfillment casts new light onto the Scriptures to which it is closely linked. The Old Testament is essential if we want to meet and know the risen Christ; we cannot bypass it. Fulfilled in Christ, it is at the heart of the New Testament witness and the Church's life. In the Gospel of Luke 24:46–48, the Church's mission to preach conversion and forgiveness of sins is itself a fulfillment of Scripture in continuity with the Easter event.

THE SYNTHETIC-DOXOLOGICAL CRITERION

The synthetic-doxological criterion unifies all biblical testimony around the Easter event of the new covenant and around the life of the Son, which from its beginning to its end tells the story of God. As we might imagine, this criterion gives special weight to those biblical texts that best help us come to know Christ. Without yielding to the temptation to create a canon within the canon and treat certain biblical books as more important than others, we should remember that, as Origen put it, "the Gospels are the first fruits of Scripture."[86] In the *Dei Verbum* we read: "among all the inspired writings, including those of the New Testament, the Gospels have a special place, and rightly so, because they are our principal source for the life and teaching of the incarnate Word, our Savior" (*DV* 18).

We do not need to choose a biblical text—say, one of the Gospels or the Pauline "gospel"—and then call that text the source of the "pure" gospel and measure other texts in the canon against it. We simply need to remember that we read Scripture to learn about Christ, and that the fourfold testimony of the Gospels gives us what we need to know him. But the reader who believes in him will search the whole Bible for ways to know him better.

We need to listen carefully to all of Scripture (cf. Rev. 22:18–19; Deut 4:2) and look for the consensus between the old and new covenants, so as to glimpse Christ's face there. Only if we understand the Bible as a Christ-centered whole will we see that difficult texts like the so-called "cursing" or "imprecatory" Psalms are not hazardous stumbling blocks, but bricks firmly cemented into the one biblical building that is Christ's body and Christological prophecy. Even these psalms are subject to the hermeneutical principle set down by Jesus (in Luke 24:44, "everything written about me in the law of Moses, the prophets, and the psalms must be fulfilled"). We should read them as bits of the full biblical mosaic, and we should note the ways in which the light of the Easter event shows them to be prophecy and prefiguration of Jesus's passion and death. According to this understanding, the curses that the psalmist invokes upon evildoers and enemies actually fell upon the suffering Servant, Jesus Christ, in his passion and death on the cross—and through Christ, God took these curses upon himself. If we read these Psalms together with Isaiah 53 and the Gospel Passion accounts, we will be able to see them as Passion prophecies. They also speak of shame, something without which Jesus's death cannot be understood. He died a criminal's death and was "numbered with the transgressors" (Isa. 53:12).

The psalmist begs God to eradicate the power of evil, and so another way in which we can pray these "cursing psalms" is to hear the psalmist's pleas for eradication of evil as directed toward ourselves—that is, against the evil and sin that are in us, and against the enemy at work in us. By praying like this we are, so to speak, grafted by grace into the new covenant through the blood of Christ, who died for our sins. These and other biblical texts that we may find harsh or scandalous are absorbed into the scandal of the cross and become opportunities for us to know God's love for us while we were, and are, sinners (cf. Rom. 5:6–11). They give us an opportunity to experience God's mercy, which came at a high cost.

Exodus 2:11–22 tells the story of how Moses killed an Egyptian, was condemned to death by Pharaoh, and escaped to Midian. Let's call this narrative the beginning of Moses's "passion." The Acts of the Apostles retells the story (7:23–29, 35) in a way that highlights the refusal of Moses's ministry of reconciliation by his fellow

Hebrews (the verb *synallassein*, Acts 7:26; cf. Exod. 2:13–14). In Stephen's speech in Acts, the Exodus passage is used as an example of how God's people disobeyed and rejected a messenger God had sent—and this refusal culminated in the death of the Righteous One (cf. Acts 7:52). For Acts, the "passion of Moses" prefigures the passion of Christ.

A passage of the Letter to the Hebrews (11:24–28) also interprets Exodus 2:11–22 rather freely, concentrating on how Moses "refused to be called a son of Pharaoh's daughter . . . [and refused] to enjoy the fleeting pleasures of sin" (Heb. 11:24–25). Hebrews' interpretation then takes a directly Christological turn: "He considered abuse suffered for the Christ to be greater wealth than the treasures of Egypt" (Heb. 11:26). Moses's passion experience is understood by the author of Hebrews to be direct participation in Christ's shame, just as the holy ones who come after Christ share in his shame (cf. Heb. 10:33; 13:13). When Moses left Egypt, he "persevered as though he saw him who is invisible" (Heb. 11:27)—suggesting that Christ is already present in a mysterious way in the Old Testament (cf. 1 Cor. 10:4).

The two New Testament excerpts we have considered, from Acts and from Hebrews, both aim to help readers see the face of Christ in the book of Exodus and find in it a prophecy of the Cross. As Evagrius Ponticus said, "The Old Testament preaches Christ crucified."[87]

THE SYNCHRONIC AND DIACHRONIC UNITY OF GOD'S PEOPLE

The process by which we come to see events in the Old Testament as relevant today is based on the fact that God's eternal word is always addressed to Israel, which sees itself as a unity in time and space. The word regards Israel as a collective unity, and it regards each individual. The concept of corporate personality (H. W. Robinson), which points to how God and the people belong to each other in covenant, makes God's word an entity that speaks to all the people gathered together as one (Neh. 8:1)—and the same word speaks to each individual as a member of the community. This is why the value of personal *lectio divina* reaches beyond the individual to the church. Because the one God's eternal Word is made known both in the prophets and in the Son, Christians can see God's people Israel as their ancestors (cf. 1 Cor. 10:6). Divided though they may be, the two peoples are still called to form God's one eschatological community. The many people who have lived since Jesus's time are also together in diachronic and synchronic unity.

We should keep this in mind during our spiritual reading of Scripture. It can be very helpful to learn about traditional Jewish biblical interpretation, such as the *Targum* tradition (Aramaic translation and glosses of the Hebrew text). This can help us better understand the New Testament, but comparing postbiblical Jewish interpretation of the Bible with the Bible itself can also give us a better sense of the otherness of God's holy people, onto whom we as Christians have been grafted.

It is also useful to consult ancient versions of the Bible, especially the Septuagint (LXX), which was the Church's Bible during its first four centuries, and Jerome's Vulgate. This is a practical way to experience the hermeneutical power of tradition. Augustine notes that capable readers (*scienter legentibus*) can profit spiritually when they compare different translations of the same biblical passage. He takes as an example Isaiah 7:9, which in the Vulgate follows the Hebrew text ("If you do not believe, you will not stand fast"). But in the Septuagint, the same text is translated as, "If you do not believe, you will not understand."[88]

Consulting different versions of the Bible can also be a gesture of ecumenical openness, a way for us to become more familiar with other ancient and modern Christian denominations as we uncover spiritual treasures hidden in the text. For example, in the ancient Syriac version (known as the Peshitta) of the book of Psalms, each psalm has a "title" that gives us a clue as to how to read it spiritually. The title given to Psalm 1 ("Blessed are those . . .") calls to mind Matthew's Beatitudes, and the title of Psalm 2 highlights that aspect of the psalm which is a prophecy of Christ's passion and of the calling of the Gentiles.

Finally, if we truly want to understand the Bible spiritually, we need to know something about how different biblical texts are used in the liturgies of different churches. This is because it is in the liturgy that biblical texts keep living and being enriched with meaning by Christian communities. The liturgy, especially the Eucharistic liturgy, is the place where Scripture deploys its full capacity to bring us into relationship with Christ. A passage of Gregory the Great conveys the hermeneutical value of a community setting, especially a liturgical one:

Many things in sacred Scripture that I could not understand alone, I came to understand when I was in the
presence of my brothers (*coram fratribus meis positus
intellexi*). . . . I realized it was thanks to them that I
received this ability to understand.[89]

SCRIPTURE AND COMMUNITY

As I understand the passage cited above, Gregory the Great is
telling us that another hermeneutical key for understanding the
Bible is concrete, day-by-day community living. Exegesis *in ecclesia*
means, first of all, living with others and being a church community. When we live life concretely in *koinonia*, over time we gain the
sort of insight and discernment into things human and spiritual that
will allow us to live even more fully—and biblical texts are, after
all, witnesses to lives fully lived. Community living can become an
experience of the Word:

. . . (t)he Holy Scriptures lie open to us with greater
clearness and as it were their very veins and marrow are
exposed, when our experience not only perceives but
actually anticipates their meaning, and the sense of the
words is revealed to us not by an exposition of them but
by practical proof.[90]

Paul Ricoeur also noted that interpretation has a "communal
character," and stressed that "the individual work of exegesis is
always done with an interpretive community in view."[91]

This is why Scripture is not a matter of "private interpretation" (2 Pet. 1:20): it has two complementary *loci exegetici*, a community's liturgies and the daily realities of Christian life. The Bible was itself produced by church communities, and this means that all members of the church (*christifideles omnes* or "all the Christian faithful," *Dei Verbum* 25) are called to be *subjects* in its spiritual interpretation (C. Kannengiesser). Biblical interpretation is not the prerogative of specialists, and no one can claim to hold the keys to it in an exclusive sense. It is for every baptized person. When we immerse ourselves in Scripture on a daily basis, we have a chance to renew our baptismal immersion and strengthen ourselves in our Christian calling.

SCRIPTURE AND MARTYRDOM

Inspired Scripture needs readers who, in the obedience of faith, will let themselves be invested with the Word's power and the *dynamis* of the Spirit. Spiritual reading leads us to give witness (*martyria*) to a Presence. Its natural fulfillment is martyrdom, in the sense of giving our lives in love.

In the second century CE, Rabbi Akiva experienced his own martyrdom as a way of living out fully what the *Shema* asks: "You shall love the Lord your God with all your life" (Deut. 6:5). As executioners were stripping flesh from his body with combs, Rabbi Akiva recited the *Shema*. His disciples tried to interrupt him, but he said,

> All my days I have been troubled by this verse, 'with all
> your life', [which I interpret,] 'even if He takes your life'. I
> said: When shall I have the opportunity of fulfilling this?
> Now that I have the opportunity, shall I not fulfill it?[92]

The Word that has brought light to our lives brings us through death to life. Jesus made the cross a place where he could fulfill Scripture by loving the Father with all his heart, strength, and life until the last breath (B. Gerhardsson), and by loving his neighbor more than himself: "It is finished" (John 19:30). He allowed Scripture to deploy all of its spiritual power in him, the power of resurrection.

CHAPTER 5

LISTENING

I f we want our time spent with the Bible to be productive, we need to listen intensely, with a "listening heart" (*lev shomea*, 1 Kgs. 3:9). The entire Bible is predicated on the fact that God speaks and people listen. People in the Bible walk by faith and not by sight, because listening is the only way to an encounter with the living God. Israel, God's people, is in essence a community of listeners (see especially Deuteronomy and Jeremiah), and so is the church. The Greek word *ecclesia* means assembly—a group of people brought together by God's word and gathered around the risen, living Christ, who is God's definitive word to humanity. The command to listen is central in both the Old and New Testaments because without listening there can be no covenant.

In Exodus, Moses is called to Mount Sinai, where God asks him to tell Israel: "You have seen what I did to the Egyptians, and how I bore you on eagles' wings and brought you to myself. Now therefore, if you *listen* to my voice and keep my covenant, you shall be my treasured possession out of all the peoples. Indeed, the whole earth is mine, but you shall be for me a priestly kingdom and a holy nation" (Exod. 19:3–6). The people are freed for communion, so that they and God can belong to one another. This happens when they listen to the Torah given on Sinai: "Listen to my voice, and do all that I command you. So shall you be my people, and I will be your God" (Jer. 11:4). This command remains in the New

Testament as a command to listen to "the Son" (Matt. 17:5, Mk. 9:7, Lk. 9:35) who is the mediator of a new covenant "not of letter but of spirit" (2 Cor. 3:6). Jesus says, "Blessed . . . are those who hear the word of God and obey it" (Lk. 11:28), and to the disciples, "Blessed are . . . your ears, for they hear. Truly I tell you, many prophets and righteous people longed . . . to hear what you hear, but did not hear it" (Matt. 13:16–17; cf. Lk. 10:23–24). The author of Revelation extends the beatitude to those people who read and hear Scripture: "Blessed is the one who reads aloud the words of the prophecy, and blessed are those who hear and who keep what is written in it" (1:3).

A dialogical structure is built into Scripture, and so naturally listening is required, since it is part of dialogue. In Jewish and in Christian patristic tradition, it was understood that Scripture was meant to be read aloud. People in antiquity and the Middle Ages read not with their eyes alone, but "with the lips, pronouncing what they saw, and with the ears, listening to the words pronounced, hearing what is called the 'voice of the pages.' It is a real acoustical reading; *legere* means at the same time *audire*."[93] For this reason the Hebrew term *miqra* actually suits the biblical text better than do the Greek words for Scripture (*graphé*) and Bible (*tà biblía*, "the books"). *Miqra* means both reading and coming together, and it "integrates Scripture with the act of reading" by designating the biblical text as something to be read aloud and proclaimed in the liturgical assembly so that every son or daughter of Israel might listen, be taught, and put into practice the words of Torah (cf. Deut. 31:10–12). *Miqra*, consisting of the verbal root *qara* ("to call, to read") and the prefix *m-* indicating provenance, refers to the *book* that calls us out of ourselves, inviting us to go *out* and to go *toward*. When we read Scripture, we are always making an exodus and moving toward an encounter. We are entering into a dialogical relationship in which the text with its *dynamis* both asks the reader to make changes, and makes those changes possible, so that we undergo a "conversion" as a step toward communion with the Lord.

With its dialogical, relational thrust, our listening to the Word requires that we be aware of and accept the text's otherness. We must come to grips with its cultural difference and distance from us. To make sense of the text, we need to use all of the tools and methods that are available to us, in various disciplines—philological, linguistic, historical, archeological, literary, comparative—so that we can access God's word in the Bible as objectively as possible. All of this, however, remains basically instrumental and must always be joined with the faith that in a certain biblical text, as it appears now in its current version, God is speaking to me today. This means that even those who lack the resources to analyze the text can still reach a correct interpretation of it through personal effort and with the Holy Spirit resting on them, flawlessly guiding their *sensus fidei*. After all, even a historical approach to a biblical text requires that we open "our own history to the word that comes to meet us from that history. And this necessary openness to the history that speaks to us in the New Testament is faith" (H. Schlier).

LISTENING IN FAITH

Truly listening to Scripture means listening with faith. In the Bible, the Hebrew command to listen (*shema*) also means to obey.

Faith comes from what is heard (*fides ex auditu*, Rom. 10:17), and Christian life is a calling to obey faithfully (*oboeditio fidei*, Rom. 16:26). Scripture itself asks people to obey (*hypakoúein*, 2 Thess. 3:14), to listen and then act, and to begin by saying "yes" to the one who speaks through it. When Moses's mediation of the covenant at Sinai finds it full expression in the written redaction of the "book of the covenant" (Exod. 24:4), the people, upon hearing the book read aloud, answer, "All that the Lord has said, we will do and we will hear" (Exod. 24:7). That is, they will live out God's word, and as they do so they will really hear and understand it.

This same passage of Exodus tells us that when we listen to the biblical word in faith, we must become personally involved. Because the story was written down, the sons and daughters of Israel (Exod. 19:1–6 ff.) of whom the text speaks are not only people who lived in the past. All of the text's future readers are included, if they listen faithfully to the words of the story and allow the always-current event of God's word to happen in their lives by entering into covenant with their Lord. Reading Scripture is prophetic mediation that brings us into the covenant so that we can live in it. The really serious question is not how to explain Scripture, but how to find our way into it. And "the world of the Bible is a world into which we enter by entrusting ourselves to it: 'We will do and we will listen'" (Jean-Pierre Sonnet). It is because the biblical language is itself a language of faith that we must make our reading of it an act of faith. The text "binds those who speak it, and in so doing fully and trustingly hand themselves over, to the revealing Word." (J. Ladrière)

The confession that Christ died and rose as it appears in the first letter to the Corinthians (15:3–5), the Easter *kerygma* that is the

New Testament core of Christian faith, is a language event that communicates more than what happened. It also communicates the way in which this event is received and made freshly operative through its re-enunciation in faith (Jean-Pierre Sonnet). When Paul tells of Christ's death and resurrection in 1 Corinthians 15:3 ff., he does so by means of an enunciation in faith, bringing himself into the story (". . . lastly, he appeared to me": 1 Cor. 15:8). Paul sees himself as profoundly implicated in the event he is announcing. He also places himself into a tradition, a chain of transmission ("I announced to you what I myself received . . ." 1 Cor. 15:3–7). The Easter announcement produces itself as an event:

> The kerygmatic enunciation creates a new situation; even if it is not welcomed, it does not leave its hearers the same as they were before. God's power, shown in the resurrection, is equally manifest in the announcement of the resurrection. Christ is risen even in the *kérygma*, as Heinrich Schlier has said: "The Easter event . . . is, so to speak, doubled in its proclamation. It is irreversibly given over in the form of kerygma, refracting itself in a 'word event.'"[94]

If confessing the event is fully part of the event's reality, then we must "not separate what is united: the confessed event and the confession of the event" (A. Gesché). Readers and listeners, moved by the Spirit and bound together in a communal and church body, are those who, in faith, let the performative power of God's word— originally present in inspired Scripture—work in them. They find themselves able to re-announce that word in a forceful way, to bear witness effectively, and to live out the word.

LISTENING IN THE SPIRIT

The performative aspect of the language of faith says a great deal about the power and energy, the *dynamis* of the scriptural word, which is the Holy Spirit's own *dynamis*. This is why we need to listen to inspired Scripture in the Spirit (*Dei Verbum* 12). Every Scripture is "God-breathed" (*theópneustos*, 2 Tim. 3:16), that is, "the sacred writings . . . have the power (*dynámena*) to instruct you for salvation through faith in Christ Jesus" (2 Tim. 3:15). Scripture reveals its own unique *dynamis*, which traces a path to salvation. The Bible's value is salvific, soteriological, much more than it is pedagogical or moral or didactic. "It gives salvation through faith" (P. Beauchamp), making its hearers able to love and do good (cf. 2 Tim. 3:17). This power springs from the Spirit's action, since the Spirit pours energy into Scripture and gives salvation to those who approach it in faith. In the words of Thomas Aquinas, "The sacraments derive their efficacy from faith": and this is equally true of the sacrament of Scripture.[95] John Chrysostom exclaimed, "Great is the power of divine Scripture"[96] that "comes from the Holy Spirit,"[97] so that, enlivened by the Spirit's energy, "every word of God contained in the divine Scriptures calls us to hope in the good things of heaven."[98]

The New Testament often prefaces its Old Testament citations with the remark that the Holy Spirit "said" or "prophesied" what comes next.[99] The phenomena of biblical re-reading and interpretation were underway while the biblical text was taking shape, and were part of the processes of formation of both the Old and New Testaments—naturally enough, since the Bible is prophetic and interpreting them is a prophetic act. Scripture is human language spoken in history—"the Torah speaks the language of humans"[100]—but as a holy or sacred book (cf. 1 Mac. 12:9, 2 Mac. 8:23), it participates in God's holiness and otherness through God's own Spirit. Biblical revelation tells us that the Spirit makes communion in otherness and difference possible. The Spirit is power from on high given to us, Christ's elusive presence in the era between Easter and the parousia, and a *dynamis* that gives Christians a new personal identity. They can leave behind both the anonymity of the slave (who was called *aprósopos* or "faceless" in the ancient world) and their prior isolation to take on the identity of a son or daughter in relationship with God and others (cf. Rom. 8:15–17, Gal. 4:6–7). The written word witnesses to absence, distance, difference, and separation, in that it tells of past historical events and points to a referent that exceeds it. But the Spirit enables this word to make a presence felt in absence, intimacy in distance, and communion in the difference between the reader (or hearer) and God who, by revealing himself in Word and Spirit, left in inspired Scripture a *signum* of his revelation.

The Holy Spirit weaves together the letter and spirit of the biblical text, and guides us toward a spiritual—that is, communion-oriented—understanding of it. By the act of reading we enter into God's covenant. "What the Spirit says, we must understand according to the Spirit," Origen says, and for Jerome, "We always need the Spirit to come so that we can comment on sacred Scripture."[101]

As a work of the Spirit—like Christ's humanity, the Eucharist and the church, those other perceptible signs through which the Word shares himself with human beings—Scripture too requires that, in order to understand it, we reach its inner vitality which is of the Spirit. Only a spiritual reading of Scripture allows us to perceive in the words the Word to which they refer us. In the same way, only a spiritual understanding of Jesus' humanity, the Eucharist and the church allow us to glimpse in the Jewish rabbi, in bread and wine, in a sociological group, the reality of which these things are the sign. What presents problems for us are not these signs, which are truly signs of what they signify because the Spirit is in them, but our natural blindness, which is removed only when we remain close to the Spirit who enlivens these realities.[102]

This is a matter of scriptural intelligence. To have salvation, it is not enough to "search the scriptures" (cf. John 5:39–47). We need to have faith and be taught by the Holy Spirit: those who learn in this way become *teodidatti*, people "taught by God" (cf. John 6:45 and Isa. 54:13). Luke always associates the fulfillment of Scripture with the descent of the Spirit, and claims that deep insight into Scripture, its "opening" (the verb *dianoígo*, Lk. 24:45), both requires and leads to an opening (*dianoígo*) of the mind (Lk. 24:45), heart (Acts 16:14), and eyes (Lk. 24:31). We are drawn in very personally, as the act of listening to Scripture becomes an experience of the present Lord.

Inspired Scripture also inspires. It shows its power by making holiness blossom in the reader and bear fruit. Those who make room in themselves for the word to deploy fully its life-giving power will eventually bear witness to that power by giving their lives (*martyria*). The martyr is the quintessential "pneumatofore" or Spirit-bearer, and in the Bible, he or she confesses with undeniable force both the inspired quality of Scripture and the way that it inspires.

LISTENING DAY AFTER DAY

We need to listen to the Bible in such a way that we hear it speaking directly to us today. Consider how the Gospels came into being: they are four spiritual re-readings of the one Christ event, which took shape at different times in the midst of diverse Christian communities, each with its own cultural location. All four communities heard the Gospel of Christ as a living word of the moment, addressed to them.

In the Old and New Testaments there is a drive to "update" key events in the history of salvation, like the Exodus, so that they feel of the moment. This desire was influential in the process of forming and structuring the biblical corpus. As a vehicle of God's word, which remains forever (cf. 1 Pet. 1:25), Scripture channels the eternal gospel (cf. Rev. 14:6) and proclaims Christ who is the same yesterday and today and always (cf. Heb. 13:8). The Bible wants us to see that "whatever was written in former days was written for our instruction" (Rom. 15:4)—for us who live at the "end of the ages" (cf. 1 Cor. 10:11). We need to know how to ascend from letter (*gramma*) to spirit (*pneuma*) by climbing up the appropriate hermeneutical ladder rungs, but what is more critical than this is our stance of faith, which makes it possible for anyone, at any time in history, to feel personally assessed and challenged by Scripture. We can then submit ourselves to its guidance, let ourselves be purified, and receive from it the ability to discern the signs of the times, instead of starting with our own preconceived notions and projecting them onto the Bible.

In the biblical text, there are words designed to take the reader's present-day experience and graft it into the past of which the text speaks. The story of the covenant at Sinai, for example, starts like this:

> On the third new moon after the Israelites had gone out of the land of Egypt, on this day (*ba-yom ha-ze*), they came into the wilderness of Sinai. (Exod. 19:1)

The medieval Jewish scholar Rashi comments:

> The text should have said: on that day. What is the significance of: on this day? Is it to tell you that the words of Torah must always be new to you, as if God had given them to you this very day.[103]

Every single day, God wants his word to be our entry into the covenant. Every day we need to listen in a new way, as Psalm 95 tells us:

> O that today you would listen to his voice!
> Do not harden your hearts, as at Meribah,
> As on the day at Massah in the wilderness,
> When your ancestors tested me,
> And put me to the proof, though they had seen my work.

The Letter to the Hebrews interprets this psalm by taking "today" to mean "every day, as long as it is called 'today'" (Heb. 3:12–13). Each "today," Christians need to stay alert and encourage each other not to let their hearts harden in sin. The Catholic liturgy of the hours has its own way of keeping Psalm 95 current: it is prayed every morning.

LISTENING AS PRAYER

As we read the Bible, our listening should turn into prayer: ". . . prayer should accompany the reading of sacred scripture, so that it becomes a dialogue between God and the human reader" (*Dei Verbum* 25). Listening is how this dialogue begins. Then, as we expose ourselves to the text and apply it to our lives, new life is breathed into the Bible and the result is genuine theology: not so much speaking *about* God as speaking *to* God, answering his word. Augustine tells students of the Bible that they need to "recognize the various kinds of expression in holy scripture . . . notice and memorize the ways in which it tends to say things." He goes on to say about such students:

> . . . this is paramount, and absolutely vital—to pray for understanding. In the literature which they study they read that "God gives wisdom, and from his face there is knowledge and understanding" (Prov. 2:6), and it is from him too that they have received even their commitment to study, provided that it is accompanied by holiness.[104]

Since we read the Bible spiritually as a way of coming to know Christ and follow him closely by obeying his word, the hermeneutical relevance of praying the biblical text is clear. It is about coming to understand through prayer, and it is especially about praying so that our whole self enters into dialogue with God.

LECTIO DIVINA AND THE MEANINGS OF SCRIPTURE

We listen so that we can journey from letter to spirit. We use all of the interpretive tools that are available so that we can better understand the will and purpose of the God who speaks in the text, and obey in faith. As we listen, we uncover different strata of meaning in the biblical text. In both Judaism and Christianity, there is the tradition of the "four senses of Scripture." The Jewish exegetical tradition started with a basic distinction between letter and spirit and then elaborated upon this, keeping in mind that the Bible is fundamentally unified just as God is one. The idea is that as we read, we can go more deeply into the text in stages. This pattern turns up in medieval Christian exegesis with the modifications we would expect. There we find the four senses of Scripture: the *literal*, the *allegorical* (or *spiritual*), the *tropological* (or *moral*), and the *anagogical*.

When we read spiritually today, we look to gain some sense of a biblical text's historical significance, and at the same time we ask what it reveals to us now and especially what it tells us about Christ. This awakens an ethical response in us as Christians. Finally, we seek entry to the text's contemplative and eschatological dimensions. In our own practice of *lectio divina* we will find that we move naturally through these four levels. We start with the historical-literary level of the text (*lectio*) and then go deeper into its revelatory dimension, where the face of Christ can be glimpsed (*meditatio*). Here we enter into a dialogue that engages and transforms our life (*oratio*). We come to share God's *makrothymia*, his gaze that takes in all human realities, and we hope for the eschatological fulfillment of the Kingdom, when we will meet face to face the Lord for whom we have searched in Scripture (*contemplatio*).

Spiritual reading is a theological activity in that it awakens and nourishes faith, hope, and love in us, and focuses these around the mystery of Christ. The tropological sense of Scripture, in which we come to see our own lives as part of salvation history, "has nothing to do with morality in the narrow, abstract sense this word tends to have in our vocabulary" (M.-J. Rondeau). Rather, it has to do with seeing human ethical action as part of the full becoming of the covenant, which is summed up in life in Christ. Spiritual hermeneutics unifies revelation and ethics in openness to God's otherness made manifest in Christ, and in openness to the otherness of people around us, in whom Christ can be recognized.

One of the most important moral tasks to which spiritual reading leads us is the "transforming of our gaze." This takes place mostly when we pray: certainly during the liturgy, but even more so when we pray by ourselves, in secret, alone with the Father. Prayer is the first use of Scripture in the Church.

To get a sense of what spiritual reading looks like, and how we can uncover the four senses in a biblical passage, let's take a look at Psalm 2.

1. Historically speaking, this is an ancient royal psalm for the coronation ceremony of a Davidic king. It evokes the turmoil and intrigue surrounding royal succession (vs. 1–3), which comes to an end when the new king takes the throne (vs. 4–6). During the enthronement rite, the king publicly announces the decree that gives his power its divine legitimacy ("You are my son, today I have begotten you," v. 7). With the scepter he has received, he makes an imprecatory gesture, shattering vessels that bear the names of enemy nations (vs. 8–9). Finally, his subjects and representatives of foreign nations pay him homage (vs. 10–12).

2. On a spiritual level, the son whom God has begotten today (v. 7) is Jesus, the Messiah who suffered the passion at the hands of the "peoples and nations" of Israel (cf. Acts 4:25–26). God raised him (cf. Acts 13:30–33) and gave him the name of Son, which is above all names (cf. Phil. 2:9), and reveals him to be higher than the angels (cf. Heb. 1:5).

3. The text invites the reader to acknowledge the lordship of the risen and living Christ today. We are called to live more fully

the vocation into which we were baptized, that of being sons and daughters of God. With the presence of Christ's Spirit guiding us—since he is the Son who is not ashamed to call us brothers and sisters (cf. Heb. 2:11)—we can enter into the psalm's I–you dialogue (*ani-atta*, v. 7) and answer "Abba" (Gal. 4:6, Rom. 8:15) to God when he says to us, "You are my son" (v. 7).

4. These biblical words have been fulfilled in Christ, but they remain an eschatological promise for Christians. It is still a struggle for us to let Christ reign fully in our lives. Only in the heavenly Jerusalem will "those who conquer . . . inherit these things. . . . I will be their God and they will be my children" (Rev. 21:7). Only in the Kingdom will Christ exercise his universal sovereignty, because that is when the last enemy, death, will finally be destroyed (cf. 1 Cor. 15:26), and he will "shepherd the peoples (Ps. 2:9 LXX) with a rod of iron" (Rev. 2:27, 12:5, 19:15).

PART TWO

LECTIO DIVINA
IN THE
CHURCH

CHAPTER 6

HOW THE BIBLE HAS
BEEN READ

As we continue to describe an approach to Scripture that can lead us to an encounter with Christ, God's definitive word to humanity, it will help to look very briefly at the different ways people have read the Bible over the course of its history.

A VERY BRIEF HISTORY OF BIBLICAL INTERPRETATION

Within the Bible itself we learn about the early history of how it was read. When prophets passed on the word of God, it had lasting force for people. They heard it as transcending the situations in which it was spoken, and so later prophets reread and re-interpreted it (for example, Second Isaiah re-interpreted First Isaiah, and Third Isaiah reread Second Isaiah). The saving event accomplished by God in his people's exodus from Egypt came to be seen as a paradigm for God's saving intervention throughout history. It was given new applications—that is, reread and rewritten—in later eras (for example, Wisdom 10–19 is a reflection on Exodus). The Old Testament is full of examples of how the Bible interprets itself, examples of intertextuality through quotation and allusion. There are also examples of midrashic interpretation within the Bible, that is, biblical passages that update the meaning of an earlier passage or event to fit a new context. Derived from the verbal root *d r sh*, meaning "to seek out" or "to investigate," the term *midrash* eventually became a technical term for a Jewish method of studying Scripture and the products of this study, namely midrashic commentaries or collections. The interpretation of the Old Testament in the New can be seen as a sort of midrash, with the basic difference being that for a Christian, one's ultimate reference point is not Torah as in Judaism, but Jesus Christ, who becomes the key for interpreting all passages of Scripture. New Testament authors made use of many Jewish exegetical techniques that were popular at the time: for example, doctrinal-narrative expositions based on a biblical text (Matt. 22:23–32, corresponding to *midrash aggadah*); and the derivation of normative principles from a passage of Torah (Matt. 19:5–6, corresponding to *midrash halakhah*). In Paul, we find cases of *a fortiori* reasoning and deduction by analogy, two of seven exegetical measures (*middot*) attributed to Rabbi Hillel, who lived until approximately 20 CE. Paul always treats the Old Testament as a treasure trove of types, figures, symbols, and prophecies that find their antitype, reality, and fulfillment in Jesus of Nazareth, the Messiah (1 Cor. 10:1–4, Gal. 4:21–31). This approach laid the foundations for typological and allegorical interpretation of Scripture, widely used by the church fathers.

Building upon the Pauline dichotomy of letter and spirit (cf. 2 Cor. 3:6), Origen directed Christian interpretation of the Bible toward the search for a *spiritual* meaning concealed behind the *literal* meaning of the biblical text. This approach obviously assumes the theological conviction that the Bible is inspired. As we said earlier,

Origen identified three layers of meaning in Scripture: a literal or historical meaning, a moral meaning (related to a biblical text's practical, ethical application), and a mystical meaning (related to the mystery of salvation history, fulfilled in Christ, and the realities of faith). This was the starting point for the doctrine of the *four senses of Scripture* developed by medieval interpreters. A couplet by Augustine of Dacia (1200s CE) sums up this schema of gradual penetration into the meaning of a biblical text:

> Littera gesta docet, quid credas allegoria,
> Moralis quid agas, quo tendas anagogia.

The literal meaning tells us about events that took place, about history (*littera gesta docet*); the allegorical or spiritual meaning expresses what we have faith in and leads us to the mystery veiled behind the text's more obvious meaning (*quid credas allegoria*). The moral or tropological meaning concerns our lives on the level of spiritual practice (*moralis quid agas*). The anagogical, or eschatological, meaning points to how the believer's hope reaches out toward ultimate realities (*quo tendas anagogia*). We should perhaps clarify that there are not really four meanings per se, but a single meaning grasped at different levels of depth.

In the Middle Ages people took a variety of approaches to reading the Bible. *Lectio divina* was a sapiential, or wisdom-seeking, approach that was about coming to know and love Christ through contact with the biblical text, and it thrived especially in monastic environments. There was also the scholastic approach to the Bible, which reached the height of its popularity at the turn of the thirteenth century. It interpreted and used the biblical text to underpin specific theological affirmations. Scholasticism involved a technical way of reading the Bible that paid close attention to the literal meaning of the text, often taking this to be the only meaning foundational for theology (for example, in Thomas Aquinas). But from the fourteenth century on, Christian interpretation of the Bible, which was largely allegorical and spiritual, took these tendencies to their logical extremes. The historical aspect of the text faded from view, and interpreters became increasingly abstract, fanciful, and artificial in inventing allegories, to the point that the quality of spiritual interpretation deteriorated. This opened the door to the modern era of biblical interpretation.

Modern interpretation was marked by a rediscovery of the literal meaning of the text, and this is still a priority today. Many factors led to this re-evaluation. The invention of printing (fifteenth century) quickly made it possible for many readers to encounter the Bible "face to face" in a way that had not been possible before. During the Reformation, Christians called for a return to Scripture as a way of purifying the Church, many of whose customs had become corrupt. The humanists urged readers to return to the sources by learning ancient languages (for example, the Latin Bible was used throughout the medieval period, but in the 1400s Lorenzo Valla called for a return to the Greek Bible). Some scholars, influenced by the development of modern scientific thought and by a growing historical consciousness, took the "sacred text" of the Bible out of its religious and ecclesial context and studied it alongside other ancient texts. These are only some of the factors that gave rise to historical and literary biblical criticism in the seventeenth and eighteenth centuries.

In this period we witness the birth of the historical-critical method (or, perhaps better, "methods" in the plural), still widely used today. A document of the Pontifical Biblical Commission called *The Interpretation of the Bible in the Church* calls this method indispensable for a "right understanding" of Scripture. Its goal is to try to shed light on the historical processes through which the biblical text was produced, its evolution over time, and so on. It is called "critical" because it makes use of the most objective scientific criteria available to reconstruct the text and then analyze it with linguistic and literary methods. In this analysis, scholars identify textual units and doublets, evaluate a text's literary genre, determine what previous elements (e.g., sources) contributed to the final text, what the final redactor contributed, and so on. The goal of this method is to find out what the text means, as far as this is possible.

Since any method that achieves dominance risks becoming an idol, and since no one method can do justice to the immensely rich and complex biblical text, many other approaches have arisen in the last few decades. Some of the most popular of these are synchronic methods, which study the biblical text as it appears in its final redacted form. These are generally literary approaches and include rhetorical analysis, narrative analysis, and semiotic analysis, among others. Particularly interesting is the canonical approach, which takes its inspiration from Jewish interpretive tradition (the cultural and religious world in which the Hebrew Bible was given its final form, in which Jesus lived, and in which the New Testament was written). Also important is reception history, which studies how the Bible has been read over the course of its history and the impact it has had on society. Still other methods of biblical interpretation have been influenced by the social sciences (sociology, cultural anthropology, psychology and psychoanalysis, and other disciplines).

IF GOD SPEAKS, A BELIEVER IS SOMEONE WHO LISTENS

The Bible's theological foundation is that God *speaks*. This is the divine act that sets everything in motion, and so God's partner is a person who listens. As we have seen, the Bible attests that listening is what makes Israel God's people. Listening creates a bond of belonging and is a doorway to the covenant. In the New Testament, listening is directed toward the person of Jesus, the Son of God: "This is my Son, the Beloved; with him I am well pleased; listen to him!" (Matt. 17:5 and elsewhere). Scripture contains a call; it asks its reader to be both a listener and a responder. To read the Bible is to make an exodus toward a place of meeting, to open ourselves to a revelation, to enter into a dialogue that can only take place if we listen. A believer is a listener by definition. As I listen, I acknowledge that the speaker is present, and I am drawn into his or her presence. I make room in myself for the other's indwelling, and I choose to trust the speaking other. The Gospels tell us to pay attention to what we hear (cf. Mk. 4:24) and *how* we hear (cf. Lk. 8:18), because we *are* what we hear. The Bible wants to craft a certain kind of person—one who has a "listening heart" (1 Kgs. 3:9). It is really with our hearts that we listen, that is, with our whole selves: listening forges our deepest selves into what they are. As we listen to the Word, our selves become a welcoming of the Other. We do not just listen to biblical verses; we engage in Spirit-guided discernment to find God's word, with faith and in the Holy Spirit. This takes us back once more to liturgy and *lectio divina*.

LITURGY

The Bible is a book that belongs to a people and is for a people. It is an inheritance, a "testament" left to readers who do what the authors once did by living out the written salvation story in their own lives. The people and the book are in a relationship of mutual belonging. The Bible is nothing without its people, but they, too, cannot go forward without the book, since they find in it their reason for being, their vocation and identity. The liturgy is the place where this mutual belonging of people and Bible, which really means the belonging of God's people to God through the covenant, is celebrated. The liturgy is also the place where the Bible is received, or better, it is the community gathered in liturgical assembly that receives the Bible. Here, Luke 4:16–21 (where Jesus reads a scriptural passage liturgically in the Nazareth synagogue, and then gives a sermon) is theologically and anthropologically significant. What happened in Nazareth happens every time the word of God is proclaimed in a liturgy. The scriptural text is read and announced to be a living word today, for a gathered community ("Today this scripture has been fulfilled in your hearing," Luke 4:21)—that is, a community brought together by God's word, a listening community, the *ekklesia*. During this assembly, a living reader lends his body to the book so that it can be heard as a meaningful word today, one spoken directly to *this* community. The reader opens the book with his hand, lets his eyes fall on the text, opens his mouth to speak and gives his own voice to Scripture— and what is written becomes a living word for today. It is the Spirit who, having presided over the process by which the Word became a book, now presides in the liturgy over the transformation of writing into Word ("The Spirit of the Lord is upon me," Luke 4:18). The Spirit's life-giving action allows God's word to sound in the gathered assembly and be the basis for liturgical action.

The need for the Spirit to be present when the Word is proclaimed liturgically is powerfully expressed by the Eucology of Serapion (fourth century). This anaphora, or Eucharistic prayer, follows Alexandrian tradition by invoking the Holy Spirit twice, in a double *epiclesis*: once before the readings, and once after the homily. These invocations are made so that the Spirit will guide the presider in the prophetic task of understanding, proclaiming, and breaking the word of God to hand to the assembly, and also so that the gathered community will receive the Word faithfully, understanding its worth. In liturgy—especially Eucharistic liturgy—there is a resurrection of Scripture as Word, so that when we read Scripture in a liturgical setting, we step into an Easter dynamic. In this liturgical setting there are four constituent elements: texts from the canonically received Bible are read, these texts are proclaimed to be God's living word for today, they are spoken to an assembly that sees them as the key to its own identity, and all of this takes place under a presiding guarantor who attests to the foundational authenticity of what is read.

The liturgical assembly is able, because of the Holy Spirit, to listen to Christ speaking, "since it is he himself who speaks when the holy scriptures are read in church" (*Sacrosanctum Concilium* 7). The people stand in front of Christ who "is still proclaiming his gospel" (ibid., 33); they allow God to enter into a covenant with his people and be in their midst. Scripture and liturgy join forces to achieve their shared goal, the deepest aspiration of the word of God—to bring people into dialogue with the Lord. The word that comes forth from the mouth of God, and to which Scripture is a witness, returns to God in the form of the people's prayerful answer (cf. Isa. 55:10–11). This is why the book of Psalms is placed at the center of the Hebrew Bible: the Psalms express, in Israel's worship and liturgy, the people's response to God's action in history and the world around them. Liturgy is deeply dialogical: God gathers his people, the reading of Scripture evokes God's saving actions in history, and the assembly answers, thanking the Father and invoking his kindness. Just as the Word finds its home in the liturgy, so the liturgy allows it to be born anew as the Word shows itself to be living, relevant, effective, and able to guide people into the covenant. The liturgy's dialogical structure meets the Bible's dialogical purpose, which the Song of Songs shows us so clearly.

LECTIO DIVINA

Origen speaks of *theia anagnosis* or "divine reading" as early as the third century, but we find the richest summary of this art of listening to the Word in the medieval writer Guigo the Carthusian:

> One day when I was busy working with my hands I began to think about our spiritual work, and all at once four stages in spiritual exercise came into my mind: reading, meditation, prayer, and contemplation (. . .) Reading is the careful study of the Scriptures, concentrating all one's powers on it. Meditation is the busy application of the mind to seek with the help of one's own reason for knowledge of hidden truth. Prayer is the heart's devoted turning to God to drive away evil and obtain what is good. Contemplation is when the mind is in some sort lifted up to God and held above itself, so that it tastes the joys of everlasting sweetness.[105]

Lectio divina, whether by ourselves or in community, requires a context of faith and prayer. We start in silence, confessing our faith that the Lord is speaking to us today through the biblical page. We invoke the Holy Spirit and open ourselves in humility to his action, because insight into the text is a Spirit-led event, not an intellectual pursuit. Study can be part of *lectio divina*, especially since *meditatio* is not introspection or psychological self-analysis but is an exploration of the text's meaning intended to bring us to its main theological message or *kerygma*. Tools can be useful here, such as the notes in our Bible, a commentary, or a Bible dictionary. From the page we have read and heard, we go on to seek the divine presence through prayer and contemplation. This is similar to what happens in Luke 4:16–21: there is a smooth transition from reading the biblical text (Jesus reads from the scroll of the prophet Isaiah) to gazing upon the person of Christ ("The eyes of all in the synagogue were fixed on him"). Just as *lectio divina* opens with prayer, it leads back into prayer. Whether thanksgiving or adoration, praise or asking for what we need, silently contemplating Christ's presence or seeking and invoking that presence, it will always be a prayer inspired by the word we have heard and meditated.

Once we have read the biblical text in our *lectio divina* and have found the Word, we go on to read ourselves and our lives in light of that Word. This brings us to an experience of unification: between faith and daily life, between our personal prayer and the liturgy, between our interiority and our social commitments. Even in the Bible itself, we experience unity between the Old and New Testaments. One goal of *lectio divina* is to understand the unity of the Scriptures in light of the basic Christian hermeneutical key found in the Bible itself: Christ, who died and rose, is God's definitive Word to human beings. There can be no fulfillment without the promise, but the fulfillment does not render the promise void—instead, it points toward an eschatological fulfillment. Fulfillment in Christ becomes promise in Christ. Christ, who died and rose "according to the scriptures" (1 Cor. 15:3–4), that is, according to "the law of Moses, the prophets, and the psalms" (Lk 24:44), does not bring Old Testament prophecy to a close. He gives it new meaning by turning it so that it points toward the Kingdom, where God's plan to save humanity is truly fulfilled.

INTERPRETING THE BIBLICAL TEXT

The Bible is a plural book. It is a library of books that were compiled in different places and eras, written in three different languages (Hebrew, Greek, and some Aramaic), and that feature a variety of literary genres (letters, poems, annals, novellas, and more). We read today from a tremendous cultural distance. The otherness of the text may feel overwhelming. In this case, we should come to the Bible as we would approach a person we want to get to know better. We listen to learn things about that person's past, and to know what her hopes and desires are, so that we can start a true conversation and get to know each other. I cannot talk over my conversation partner, but I cannot let him or her silence me either. This is how it is with the Bible: there are many things we can and must do to get to know it well, and to let ourselves be known. In the process we need to avoid manipulating the word too roughly. Since the Bible is a book in which God's word is contained and passed on in human words, it always has a theological element (faith in God who acts in history and who, in the New Testament, reveals himself fully in the Messiah Jesus of Nazareth), as well as a cultural dimension that varies depending on who the author of a given text was, and when and where it was written. The cultural dimension includes such things as literary genres, stylistic choices, and the influence of other cultures and their literatures. To interpret a passage fully, we need to use an exegetical approach, because this kind of approach takes the text's otherness seriously. At the same time, we need a spiritual hermeneutic that will bring us into relationship with the God who is speaking through human words. The effort of exegetical work is needed because of the historical character of the biblical word and the centrality of the incarnation in Christian faith.

Exegetical study has three basic components: textual criticism, literary criticism, and historical criticism. Text critics examine the biblical manuscripts that are available and try to establish by philological methods which texts are most sound. Literary critics study the linguistic and stylistic choices and compositional methods used in a given text, its structure and literary genre. They try to identify any sources the biblical author may have used, and the author's redactional strategy. And then there is the task of trying to understand a text's historical setting. All of these steps, taken together, allow the text's meaning to emerge with a certain objectivity—even beyond the original author's intention, which it is often wishful thinking to imagine we can reconstruct. At this point, we must make the most genuinely hermeneutic move, which is to build a bridge between the text and our lives today.

Let us see how this process works by looking at the prologue of the third Gospel (Lk. 1:1–4). The text itself mentions four stages: first, what happened in history (1:1); second, the handing down of remembered events by eyewitnesses in Christian communities who interpreted those events in faith (1:1–2), third, the writing of the gospel accounts (1:3, but also 1:1); and finally, the offering of what has been written to recipients ("for you, most excellent Theophilus," 1:4). Reconstructing the first three of these steps in the history of a Gospel's composition is the task of exegesis: historical criticism in the case of what happened, and textual and literary criticism in the case of how the Gospels were redacted and what came before them. Once I have found out what the text says, I need to bring out what it says to me, to us, *today*: this is the task of spiritual hermeneutics.

CHAPTER 7

LECTIO DIVINA:
FOUNDATIONS AND PRACTICE

LECTIO DIVINA: FOUNDATIONS

We have given a brief overview of what *lectio divina* is and what makes it possible. We are now ready to look at the ways in which this prayerful, ecclesial method of reading the Bible is both traditional and contemporary.

We have seen how *lectio divina* is an act of reading the Bible that opens into listening to God's word, encountering the Lord who speaks through the biblical page, and entering into relationship with him. *Lectio* aims to set in motion a spiritual hermeneutic of Scripture. Only if we are initiated into the practice of reading the Bible in the Spirit can we express the renewed centrality of the Word in the Church, which otherwise will remain an empty slogan.

We have also seen how *lectio divina* is inspired by the basic principles of reading Scripture that were developed in Jewish tradition, taken up in Christianity, and handed down to us. *Lectio* is reading in faith, in prayer, in openness to the Spirit so that we come to hear God's Word calling out to us today from the biblical page.

In Christian tradition, *lectio divina* is envisioned as taking place in several steps or stages, and there are various models that describe this process. An especially influential description by Guigo II the Carthusian names four stages, *lectio-meditatio-oratio-contemplatio*. It may be helpful to see this progression today as a necessary initiation into the art of meeting the Other. It is the training of body and spirit that is asked of us so that we may enter into dialogue and relationship with the Lord who speaks through the text, and live in his presence.

Let us now begin this journey of *lectio divina*. The first step is to make an invocation of the Spirit, and enter into a climate of prayer in which we prepare to leave ourselves behind and seek the face of Christ, whom we confess in faith to be present in Scripture. It is a good idea to read through an entire book of the Bible, several verses per day, so that we do not just pick and choose passages as we please. We begin our reading in search of an objective and correct comprehension of the "letter" of the text. This means trying to avoid purely subjective interpretations so that we can access the text in its otherness, come to know it with objectivity as it tells us about the Lord, and come to discern the Lord who speaks to us through it.

In *meditatio*, we deepen this understanding through reflection and study, until the message of Scripture becomes clear enough to reach us as we read or listen, wounding or consoling, but always revealing Christ crucified and risen. By now Scripture is a Word addressed to me, revealing an event that has to do with me and also revealing the love of Christ, who "loved me and gave himself for me" (Gal. 2:20). *Meditatio* is like the alternating heartbeat phases of systole and diastole: we apply the text to ourselves, and ourselves to the text[106] until we start to "breathe Scripture."[107] In the space of *meditatio* I read and evaluate my personal and communal life before God and his word. I think of myself in relation to what the Word demands, so that I will be moved to act in obedience to God's word in my daily life.

Thinking is integrated with praying as I bring my personal life objectively before God, just as in the psalms of supplication. There we find the speaker "setting out his case," that is, describing his own situation in God's presence. By now, Scripture will have given me a word, one addressed to me personally, and so I enter into dialogue, *oratio*, with God and accept God's covenant, which is costly grace.

Since I have come to Scripture in faith, open to the Spirit's action, my prayer is no longer a monologue, introspective thinking, or moralistic self-examination. I have a conversation partner who is present with me in prayer, and this leads to *contemplatio*, the revelation of this Presence in ourselves. We discover that we are called to make our own bodies and lives transparent to Christ for others. In *contemplatio* we can glimpse Christ's face, first revealed by Scripture, in the faces of those around us and in the created world, because we have drawn very close to the spirit of the gospel, the breath of Christ, God's gaze and way of seeing.

Lectio divina, then, is spiritual reading of Scripture that allows the Word sent by God to accomplish its course, yielding fruit in human hearts and showing itself to be fertile (cf. Isa. 55:10–11) by making our lives holy and Eucharistic, lives of conversion (*eucharistoi ghinesthe*, "become Eucharistic," Col. 3:15). *Lectio* encircles and engages our entire being: we are challenged to think about who we really are, and then place that person face to face with God's word and receive our true identity in this relationship, this dialogue and covenant. We will have to change things about ourselves and how we live. *Lectio* is a place where choices are made, where we learn discernment and restraint. It can vitally renew the entire sphere of our work and activity from within, because it refines our interiority, how we feel and desire.

The dynamic at work in our encounter with the Lord in *lectio divina* is not all that different from the anthropological dynamic present in any interaction we have with another human being. The basic steps are the same: we make an exodus from ourselves, die to our own narcissism, listen to the other person, look closely at her face (*perscrutatio*) for a glimpse into her soul, who she is deep down. We come to know the other person when we respect how he is different and other, and when we can accept who we are in relation to him. These are the steps toward a genuine relationship between people in which freedom and love are present and an adventure of communion is possible.

There is a task for the Church here. The Church cannot ignore children who are crying out for bread, the bread of the Word. It must break this bread, hand over Scripture as the food that it is, the food that nourishes and satisfies, by teaching people to "pray the Word." The Church has the responsibility to introduce people to the art of listening to the Word by reading the Bible in the Spirit.

Passing on our faith to others *means* handing down Scripture. The traditional expression "Scripturae faciunt christianos" is a paraphrase of St. Augustine (J. Caillot), who also says that "our daily bread . . . our daily food on this earth is God's word, which is always distributed in the churches."[108]

We need to take seriously the divine-human character of Scripture, its way of bearing witness to the Incarnation because insofar as it is writing, *graphé*, it is a form of the Logos's incarnation analogous to Christ's physical body.[109]

Today more than ever, we need to read Scripture in such a way that we can harvest and hand to others its wisdom teaching, its dual nature of divine word and human word. The covenant and place of meeting shown to us in Scripture are not back in the distant past, but have everything to do with where we are now and how we live out our humanity today. We need to grasp that what Scripture announces is new at every moment, even in the first pages of Genesis, where we find what is primordial, universal, and constant in our human nature. When we allow the light of the centrality of Christ—who came into the world to bring salvation to all and teach us to live (cf. Tit. 2:11–12)—to fall on this reading, we can structure our interpretation around Jesus's testimony of how to become human, since he himself grew "in wisdom and in years, and in divine and human favor" (Lk. 2:52). The reader's human and spiritual growth can then be oriented toward reaching the full stature of Christ (cf. Eph 4.:13).

The need to read this way is all the more urgent because in the church there are impoverished readings of Scripture that do not maintain its delicate balance of divine word and human word. We encounter fundamentalist and literalist tendencies, and on the other side of the spectrum, attempts to reduce the Bible to a human book—a pious and edifying one, or a product of a certain culture or ideology. There are also Marcionite tendencies that tear Scripture in two, especially by devaluing the Old Testament in comparison with the New.

These pathologies are reminiscent of certain christological heresies in the early church, from monophysitism to Nestorianism to docetism. There are readers today who approach the text like archeologists, wanting to get to the concrete "letter" at all costs. Others are spiritually narcissistic, not accepting the text's otherness and fusing themselves with it so that it is no longer "other" at all. Or, readers focus so intensely on what the text meant in its historical context that they fail to see the text's own intention to transcend itself. We need to remember that there is an organic relationship between the literary form and the spiritual content of Scripture. The analogy between Scripture and the incarnation of Christ implies that, just as we cannot reach God or Christ's divinity by bypassing his humanity (we have to go through it), the same is true with Scripture. And, just as the Spirit presides over Christ's incarnation, the Spirit must preside over our reading of Scripture. The Spirit guides us to the fullness of truth, and to an understanding of Scripture. Without the Spirit, communion in otherness cannot take place. The breath that blows the word of God toward humans, the Spirit then summons from within us an answer to the God who speaks, and moderates the dialogue between God and us. The same Spirit who is present in Scripture and inspires readers also produces a synergy in which Scripture both grows with those who read it, and makes them grow through their contact with it.

In the light of all we have just said, it should be clear that *lectio divina* seeks to unify our life, faith, and prayer, and it also brings into unity what is human and what is spiritual, what is inner and what is exterior. In *lectio* we aim to integrate study and critical analysis of the text with a wisdom-seeking and prayerful approach, an approach in faith.

LECTIO DIVINA: PRACTICE

TIME AND SPACE

For *lectio divina* we need a quiet place where we can be alone to search for and listen to God "who is in secret" (Matt. 6:6). To prepare ourselves to hear the Word, we need to silence the many words and noises that make our heart unable to hear. We then enter into the bare essentiality of silence and solitude, distancing ourselves from all the things that assail us daily. A word with authority can only come out of silence, after we have listened intensely, meditated, reflected and thought things over carefully. We may wish to look at an icon or light a candle; in one way or another we need to prepare our body to meet the Lord, since *lectio* is not just intellectual but seeks to engage all of who we are. It is a good idea to dedicate a fixed time in our day to *lectio* and stay faithful to that time, rather than trying to squeeze in our *lectio* between our various other commitments. An hour is about the right amount of time to enter into *lectio* in a serious way, but our practice will bear fruit if we persevere day after day. The amount of time we can give will obviously depend on our schedule and other commitments.

Lectio divina builds up our *sensus fidei*, gives us the ability to discern, and is a form of ascetic training. We need to take the seed of the

Word within ourselves so that it can put down roots. Perseverance is crucial: no matter how enthusiastically we listen, our listening will remain sterile unless we keep going over time. There is also an element of spiritual struggle in *lectio*, as we fight to hold on to the Word and not let it be suffocated by the thorns of distracting desires (cf. Mk. 4:13–20). Very concretely, in *lectio divina* we make space for God's word to take control, to reign in and rule our lives. This is one more reminder that *lectio* is about far more than just studying a text: people with an intellectual nature run the risk of looking for cerebral or aesthetic pleasures in the Bible and stopping there. They tend to get excited by the brilliant ideas that come to them, or they find the text's beauty so enchanting that they do not get to benefit from its true spiritual fruit.

PRAYER

We prepare ourselves for *lectio* with silence, with an exodus from ourselves, and with prayer: we call upon the Holy Spirit with an *epiclesis* or invocation, asking the Spirit to open the eyes of our heart and give us insight into the Word. Then, to help ourselves enter into a space of listening and loving dialogue with the Lord who speaks through the biblical page, we may wish to read a section of the "Psalm of listening" (Ps. 119), which is a love duet like the Song of Songs. And so we go further into experiencing *lectio divina* as a sacramental place where we can know God's love.

LECTIO

The opening act of *lectio divina* proper is the act of reading. I think that today we need to learn and teach others to read and be in dialectical relation with the Bible, since it is such a demanding book. By the way, we should make clear that *lectio* is a reading of the Bible and nothing else. Christian tradition has at times understood it more broadly as referring to other authoritative texts one should read, such as the writings of the church fathers. But in the church, only the Bible has the unique status of sacrament of God's word. And we call this act of reading "divine" because we are reading inspired Scripture. We can certainly read other books (patristic commentaries and so forth) alongside the Bible or as spiritual reading, but the term *lectio divina* is reserved for reading Scripture.

How do I select which Bible passage to read? Either I choose a book of the Bible and read it through from beginning to end, one pericope per day, or I follow the Bible readings in the daily liturgy (I might choose one of them, such as the Gospel). With the first option, I have the enriching possibility of delving deeply into a biblical book and getting a sense of it as a whole. With the second option, my personal prayer merges with liturgical prayer. The Catholic Church's lectionary for feast days has much to offer in that a single theme unites all three readings (or at least the Old Testament and the Gospel; this is not the case in the daily lectionary). In any event, it is spiritually fruitful to choose for our *lectio* a biblical passage relevant to the current liturgical season.

If someone has little or no familiarity with the Bible, it is best to ease slowly into *lectio* by starting with a text that is both simple and foundational, such as the Gospel of Mark (followed by, for example, Exodus 1–24, the Acts of the Apostles, and then a prophetic book). Later on, the more experienced reader can approach books like Daniel, Romans, Galatians, Hebrews, and Revelation.

I have chosen a passage and I start to read. I read through my text as many as four or five times. If it is a passage I know already, I may be tempted to read superficially rather than intensively, in which case I lose much of its richness. One useful strategy here is to write out the passage by hand. This forces me to concentrate and may help me see things I had never noticed before. Those who know Hebrew and Greek can read the original text, tapping into the complexity that translations inevitably hide from view. But a good translation, or several translations side by side, is a fine place to start. There is much to be gained spiritually from using an aid like a concordance, or a book of Gospel parallels if we are reading a Gospel passage.

Even if I am doing my *lectio divina* alone in my room with the door closed, I like to read aloud so that I can actually hear the words. For the medieval fathers, it was essential to hear the *voces paginarum* (voice of the pages): listening is already prayer, already a way to take in the word and the speaker's presence.

MEDITATIO

Meditation in *lectio divina* is not Ignatian-style introspection or psychological self-analysis. It is how we get to a text's deeper meaning. We may wish to use study tools here, such as Bible dictionaries and commentaries. Even though *lectio divina* is not the same thing as studying a Bible passage, study can and should be part of it.

We need to find our way into the text despite its otherness, its vastly different cultural context and language. By taking the text's otherness seriously, we will not be tempted to read so subjectively that we end up making the text say things it does not say at all. The issue is to obey the Word rather than manipulating it. Every so often someone may accuse us of being overly academic or treating the Bible as if it had "only cultural value" simply because we are trying to respect the text's alterity, but this is not the case. If we refuse to study the Bible in a deeply investigative way, we cannot thrive either as individuals or as a community. In any case, whichever tools we use to help us understand a biblical passage, our personal effort will yield results.

ORATIO

The dialogical back-and-forth we have established with the text now becomes prayer in which I say "you" to God. Here there are no specific instructions to give. We simply follow where the Word and the Spirit lead. The Word itself shapes our prayer, whether it be intercession or thanksgiving or request or invocation. Or, we may pray in silence, in adoration, or even with the gift of tears. Sometimes it happens that we find ourselves in the aridity of the desert: the text resists all our efforts to understand it, the Word is silent, and prayer does not come. There are times like this in any real relationship, even with the Lord. He calls us out to the desert to meet him, but sometimes the desert is not a meeting place. It is just dry and exhausting. Even at times like this, we should go forward, persevere, and perhaps offer God our mute body as a way of praying without words. The Lord can tell when we want to pray.

Also, our close contact with God's word in *lectio divina* becomes most clearly effective over time. By training ourselves to listen, we are making room for the Lord in ourselves. We welcome the Word and it turns us into children of God (cf. John 1:12) and makes us capable of contemplation.

CONTEMPLATIO

Contemplation is the last "step" of this ideal ladder. We sense God's presence within us and rejoice with the "indescribable and glorious" joy of that indwelling. Bernard of Clairvaux wrote about this experience:

> I admit that the Word has also come to me (. . .) and has come many times. But although he has come to me, I have never been conscious of the moment of his coming. I perceived his presence, I remembered afterwards that he had been with me; sometimes I had a presentiment that he would come, but I was never conscious of his coming or his going. And where he comes from when he visits my soul, and where he goes, and by what means he enters and goes out, I admit that I do not know even now; as John says: "You do not know where he comes from or where he goes." (John 3:8)[110]

Contemplation is not an ecstatic state or "visions." It is the gradual transformation of our gaze so that it becomes like God's way of seeing. As this happens, we gain a spirit of thanksgiving and compassion, discernment, patience, and peace. Just as the Word points to the Eucharist, so *lectio divina* makes us Eucharistic people. We become capable of gratitude and can discern Christ's presence in others and in a variety of life situations. We know love and are able to act with *agape*. *Lectio divina* spills over into life, showing its fruitfulness in how we live.

We have now seen how *lectio divina* traces an arc from prayer to prayer. It begins with an invocation of the Spirit and opens into contemplation, thanksgiving, and praise.

CHAPTER 8

CHALLENGES DURING
LECTIO DIVINA

There is no doubt that this primacy of holiness and prayer is inconceivable without a renewed *listening to the word of God*. It is especially necessary that listening to the word of God should become a life-giving encounter, in the ancient and ever valid tradition of *lectio divina*, which draws from the biblical text the living word which questions, directs and shapes our lives.[111]

These words were written at the start of the third Christian millennium. For the first time, an apostolic letter addressed to all the faithful recommended that Christians everywhere practice *lectio divina* for the flourishing of their spiritual lives. This pressing invitation from John Paul II is still timely. Scripture is back at the center of the Catholic Church, and there is a great deal we can say today about where its value for the Church lies.

Catholics experienced a long estrangement from the Bible that ended just decades ago. Without direct contact with Scripture, they could not treat it as daily sustenance for their faith lives and their witness to the world. Of course the Catholic Church continued to live on God's word, especially in the liturgy, but that word was no longer heard, celebrated, meditated, or held in hearts in such a way as to build up the faith of individual believers and groups.

Now at the heart of the church's life once more, the Bible has reopened a wellspring that was blocked for centuries. By spending time with Scripture day after day, we can nourish our faith, discern our place among other people, and above all immerse ourselves in the *epignosis* (spiritual knowledge) of Christ and of God's mystery that will make each of us a mature (*teleios*, "perfect") believer. Today our preaching, especially in liturgical contexts, is strengthened by the Holy Scriptures and helps make God's word heard in Christian communities. The word of God is able to spread as Paul had hoped: "Pray for us, so that the word of the Lord may spread rapidly and be glorified everywhere" (2 Thess. 3:1). It is fair to say there is a hunger, a deep desire for God's word right now.

I am convinced that the most appreciable gain of Vatican II is the giving back of God's word to the people of God. Yet there are still important objectives to pursue, more than forty years after the Council's end. First and foremost, we need to be deeply aware of what spending time with Scripture, especially in *lectio divina*, can do for us. I will touch on just a few points, all of which I have discussed in other publications.[112]

READING THE BIBLE DAY BY DAY

The Bible may well be at the center of some ecclesial activities again (such as liturgy, pastoral life, and catechesis). But we cannot say the same about the daily lives of lay Catholics, since most people do not set aside time regularly to read it. Of course some priests, religious, and lay people are at ease with the Bible because of their background and training, and there are church movements whose spirituality focuses on reading Scripture. But most believers still have no personal contact with the Bible. Many families own Bibles, but treat them as decorative objects and rarely open them to pray or listen to God's word. I have also heard people express skepticism about reading the Bible daily because they think this practice is foreign to Catholic tradition. Another obstacle is that priests lacking training in reading Scripture are not able to help their parishioners in this: they do not encourage them enough and cannot offer a real introduction to the practice.

In the diverse, pluralistic, and multicultural society in which we live, with its many different religious traditions, reading the Bible matters more than ever. Christians no longer form a homogeneous group, and increasingly we live in a kind of diaspora situation. Faith can only grow deep roots in us if we stay close to the living stream of spiritual life. Few people go to daily Mass these days, and in some places there is no daily Mass at all. Christians have to provide themselves with their own food for the journey of faith, by taking the initiative to listen to Scripture. Church communities rarely spend enough time together to shape the faith of Christians and show them how to live out that faith in the world. But God's word in Scripture is there to ground us spiritually, show us how to act, help us discern the signs of the times, and teach us to pray.

People today often think of prayer more as meditation in God's presence than as dialogue with God. What can we do for people, concretely, to help them hear Scripture and meditate on it? The prayerful, meditative dimension of our contact with

Scripture is crucial for sharing our faith with future generations. Jewish communities have shown us how faith can remain alive in diaspora settings when people cherish Scripture and keep the Sabbath, a teaching learned from the Bible. In a memorable address to the Council of the Bishops' Conferences of Europe in 2001, the former Cardinal Ratzinger insisted that today as much as ever, people develop *sensus fidei* by turning to the Bible again and again: "I am convinced that *lectio divina* is the basic element that forms one's *sensus fidei*, which makes it the most important task of a bishop who teaches the faith."[113]

DIVINA ELOQUIA CUM LEGENTE CRESCUNT

The Lord's word builds up entire communities and strengthens each community member at the same time. We might say with Luke that "[t]he word of God continued to spread; the number of the disciples increased greatly" (Acts 6:7), or that God's word grows to the extent that it spreads: "The word of God grew and multiplied" (Acts 12:24; author's translation). When the Word grows, communities grow with it, because a community is the fruit that is harvested after God's effective word is planted. It is also where the Word is lived out in action. According to a patristic saying, Scripture makes Christians who they are ("Scripturae faciunt christianos"), but it is equally true that "divine messages grow with those who read them,"[114] meaning that God's word grows when the church interprets it. The church's life actually becomes a "living hermeneutic" of Scripture.

We should encourage people to practice *lectio divina* both personally and communally, wherever people gather, in congregations and Christian groups of all kinds. *Lectio* should not be left to religious communities as often happens. It can be very helpful to prepare ourselves for the Sunday Eucharist with *lectio divina;* the sermon is then like a conclusion to our own reading. *Lectio* practiced by a gathered community is rare today, but we should make more room for it. We need to make the effort and summon the courage to suggest new strategies that could work in our own communities.

The community is inseparable from Scripture, because a book is nothing without a community that reads it, and the community finds its identity and vocation in the book. Bernard of Clairvaux defines a Christian community as a mirror of the book, and the book as a mirror of the community.

WORD AND HISTORY

This brings us to the relationship between God's word and history. To understand the issues at stake, we need to consider three temptations Christians face when they read the Bible.

1. The first is *fundamentalism*, which has to do with thinking we can understand God's word without making any effort to study the Bible. This temptation arises when we ignore historical criticism and other exegetical methods and do not let the Spirit guide our interpretation. The Pontifical Biblical Commission condemned fundamentalism in the document *The Interpretation of the Bible in the Church*: "Without saying as much in so many words, fundamentalism actually invites people to a kind of intellectual suicide" (n. 2980).

2. The next temptation involves thinking that we can get to the message of a biblical passage without grappling with the letter of the text, the tough "husk" of human discourse. Here we run the serious risk of manipulating God's word, reading subjectively, and watering down the biblical text to a psychological or affective message.

3. The third temptation is being interested *only* in the history behind the text and analyzing what is on the page without seeking insight into its deeper message. The risk in this case is that we will read the Bible without asking questions about meaning.

These temptations arise when we forget that reading the Bible always requires us to travel from Scripture to life (cf. Lk. 4:16–30), and then from life back to Scripture (cf. Lk. 24:13–35). The first direction is the one Christian communities use the most, and with good reason: by putting it first, we make clear that God's word reigns in and guides our community. The Word inspires, convinces people, and brings faith into being. But we also need to make the return trip from daily life back to Scripture, by paying attention to concrete events and situations in which there might be a call, a sign given in the space and time in which we live. With this second approach, we do run the risk of exploiting God's word in an attempt to defend our prior ideological commitments. If we let this happen, the Word becomes the object of a biased interpretation and can no longer help us discern the signs of the times. Still, it is essential for us to undertake the journey from life back to Scripture, especially if we want to witness to a faith that will be relevant to those around us.

CHAPTER 9

THE CHALLENGES OF
LECTIO DIVINA

I have mentioned briefly some of the challenges of reading the
Bible and doing *lectio divina*. Let us look at several of these in
more detail.

In the decades since Vatican II, many individuals and groups have
learned to do *lectio divina*. They have seen it as a way to read the
Bible as church and grow in faith. But with the passing of time
the first sparks of enthusiasm have died away, and the journey has
begun to feel long and arduous to many.

Local congregations tend to expend more energy on pastoral
work, practical and organizational duties, and charitable endeavors
than they do on the essential task of teaching people the art of
living well. This includes showing them how to strengthen their
faith. Congregations fail to prioritize the work of helping people
understand what it means to have an inner life. The arts of personal
prayer and the spiritual struggle are not taught, and the Bible is
often neglected—especially the Gospels, through which we come
to know Jesus Christ and his centrality for Christian faith. I see a
certain disconnect today between ecclesial life and spiritual life.
This is obviously a problem for *lectio divina*, which risks either not
being understood, or ending up on a long list of things that need to
get done. The practice of *lectio* may be delegated to the parish's Bible
study group or to people who think of themselves as "Bible lovers,"

in which case it has no chance to empower, enliven, and deploy its force of innovation in the community as a whole. A congregation that doesn't make enough room for the Bible fails to express its own vocation to be *ecclesia*, an assembly drawn together by God's word proclaimed in the Eucharistic liturgy. Scripture and church are so tightly interwoven that our approach to Scripture will be seen in our ecclesiology; how we approach Scripture amounts to a profile of our church.

One problem, then, is this disconnect between ecclesial life as I have just described it and "life in the Holy Spirit." There is a related problem: many Christians have little knowledge of the things of faith. This is probably the natural outcome of living in a culture that is no longer "Christian," in the sense of no longer being steeped in Christian words and gestures. Also, the way we do religious education today is often startlingly lifeless. That Christian formation has its deficits is plain to see even when we look at people who go to church regularly—often, they have only the most basic acquaintance with Christian teaching, if that. We are facing a widespread religious illiteracy.

None of this makes *lectio divina* any easier. We want to see this faith-filled approach to Scripture flourish, in which we read the page to find ourselves in a personal relationship with a Presence. But perhaps the roadblocks actually show us a way forward. We could treat the Bible itself, primarily the Gospels, as our most valuable resource for catechism and for sharing our faith. This would help young adults in our communities grow up with a more biblically grounded and Christ-centered faith. One would hope they would also develop a sense of freedom, knowing that they can go directly to the Gospel and Jesus's life for answers. They would then start to feel, almost naturally, that *lectio divina* is a form of prayer they need. The way to start them on this path to knowing and following Christ, and understanding the challenges involved in discipleship, would be to have them read the Gospel of Mark. Then, we would use Matthew's Gospel to introduce them to the life of the church. Through Luke, they would learn about life in the Spirit and how the Gospel sheds light on everything that happens in our daily lives. And with John, traditionally called the "spiritual Gospel," they would learn about growing spiritually and in faith.

WHY READING IS HARD

We live at a time of crisis for classic books and book culture.[115] The right to information has morphed into the (perverse) myth of information, which pushes many of us to read daily publications and magazines and gulp down all the data we can find on every conceivable topic. Yet we are unable to keep ourselves reasonably up to date even on issues where we think we are "in the know." We read broadly rather than deeply and go for quantity over quality. We have sacrificed the gaining of wisdom on the altar of information harvesting, and we want it in real time whenever possible. Further, we often fail to think critically about what we take in.

Books are increasingly sidelined from people's daily lives. Reading takes time. It can't be rushed, but we tend to rush in general. Images and visual communication rule, and with television and Internet always available, people are unlikely to pick up a book and read it—after all, this is objectively harder. But with the forms of information and entertainment just mentioned we easily slide into mental laziness. Our inner selves and lives are gradually taken over, colonized, wiped off the map, and we become people who absorb things passively rather than people who create. Yet if we are aware that the book—the classic book—is a "quintessence and symbol of human life," a "primal form in which existence is summed up" (R. Guardini), then we will understand what reading is, spiritually speaking. It is about finding meaning in life. It is an event that draws in our entire selves and awakens our inner life. We read as a way of thinking things through, and in order to meet people whose personalities are more original and brilliant than ours. We read to get a better sense of who we are in light of a text, given that reader and author share one human nature. Paul Ricoeur writes:

> Contrary to the concept of *cogito* and the subject's claim to have at his disposal an immediate intuition of his existence, we understand ourselves as we pass through the great testimonies that humanity has left in works of culture. If literature had not articulated in language love and hate, ethical reflection and everything else that forms us, we would know little about it (. . .) To understand oneself before the text is not to impose one's own finite capacity of understanding on it, but to expose oneself to receive from it a larger self.[116]

The challenge of reading goes hand in hand with the challenge of activating our inner life and learning to think. Since these things are hard, starting *lectio divina* is hard. The challenges we have been talking about have a negative impact on how we see ourselves deep down, how we position ourselves inwardly as praying subjects. The traditional path of *lectio divina* has, as we have seen, the four steps of *lectio, meditatio, oratio,* and *contemplatio.* These can be summarized in two basic stages: objective (*lectio-meditatio*) and subjective (*oratio-contemplatio*). In the first stage we let the text speak so that its message can emerge; we concentrate on listening to the passage and study it to understand better. In the second stage, the subjectivity of the person at prayer comes into play. Here we think about our life and bring it into the light of the biblical text. There should be dialogue between the text's message as we have heard it and our lives. We will know that we have read well if we feel that the text is reading us. This is exactly what we will discover if we stay with our *lectio divina*: that we are being "read" by the biblical page more thoroughly than we are able to read it. To summarize, *lectio divina* is an art that can only be performed by someone who has an inner life, who knows how to think and dialogue inwardly. None of this has ever been simple, but it is especially hard today.

WHY THE BIBLE IS CHALLENGING

Reading is challenging, and the Bible is a harder book than most. Most of the reasons why can be gathered under the rubric of what I have been calling the *text's otherness.* Those of us who are Westerners are at a cultural distance from the ancient Semitic world and its ways of thinking. The Bible is filled with cultural references to situations, events, countries, peoples, habits, and customs that are foreign to us. Biblical language and poetry are distant from Western literary and poetic forms; they too point to the text's cultural distance from us, and require us to do some work if we wish to enter this different world. These issues arise when we read any ancient text, and any text from another religious or cultural context. But when people read the Bible, they see this cultural distance and other seemingly insurmountable obstacles and wonder whether they really have to read Scripture, especially the Old Testament. What relevance can it possibly have for the contemporary person? This objection is short-sighted because it makes the adjective ("contemporary") more important than the noun ("person"). The cultural differences we see in the Bible do not destroy, but enhance

> the radical unity and resemblance of all people, Eastern or Western, ancient or modern. If each of us goes down into the depths of the noun, he or she finds simply "human." This is fleshed out in history and in each person's life with many different adjectives, different levels of what is essential or accidental. A great deal of language in the Old Testament is close to what is simply, fundamentally, primally human.[117]

The text's otherness is related to every person's otherness from us. It takes work to start a relationship with any "other." In this sense, what takes place in *lectio divina* is very human; we have to make an effort to become the humans that we are. By reading with humanity we can perceive what is existential in Scripture's human language. This tells us why we need to bring our own lived experience and existential questions to Scripture as hermeneutical criteria, that is, keys to help us interpret.

This brings us to what is perhaps the question people ask most often while doing *lectio divina*: How do I apply the biblical page to my life? What meaning does this text offer me personally?

FROM THE PAGE TO OUR LIVES

The challenges in lectio divina that we have seen so far are related either to the subjective side of things (the reader's state of mind and personal life) or to objective issues (things that make the Bible inherently hard to deal with). But the real issue in *lectio divina* is bringing these two worlds together: how can I find a message for my life in this biblical passage? How do I flesh out my belief that God's word contained in Scripture is also being spoken to me right now, and to all of us? People who struggle with this respond in a number of different ways.

Some people give up, deciding that *lectio divina* is for biblical scholars and theologians whose education makes it possible for them to find eloquence in passages that the average person will never be able to decode.

Other people make their *lectio divina* moralistic, even guilt-inducing: the Bible tells me what I have to do and how I have to be, but I am not up to the task and I feel guilty. This, however, shuts down exactly what is so potentially fruitful in *lectio divina*: the opening of my heart to the contemplation of Christ's face, and all that he does to save me and free me from gazes that victimize me by focusing on my weaknesses, sins, and inadequacies.

Still others—and I think this tendency is very common—use psychology as a tool to help them apply the biblical page to their lives. They take a psychological approach such as depth psychology and try to read a biblical passage in relation to it. Here there is the serious risk that readers will spend their time and energy looking only for what they expect to find in the text, rather than opening themselves to the newness we discover when we listen carefully for the unexpected. The "humanity" of many biblical passages does reveal psychological depth, and we can and should use certain psychological concepts to help ourselves clarify what is happening in a text. But if we read a biblical text against a psychological framework, we risk diluting the Bible's revelatory message so that it ends up looking like one of many redemption myths. Paradoxically, the biblical word shows its full therapeutic power in a reader's life when it is not shackled to approaches that, while they are meant to make it more accessible, actually prevent it from being "other." Such approaches lock the biblical word inside a reader's conceptual world, the world of what he or she already knows and desires.

Another way people react to the Bible is that they decide interpretation is too much work, and they turn to a literal, often fundamentalist interpretation. This is a shortcut that goes nowhere. All it says is that the reader has rejected hermeneutical effort in favor of literalism. As Paul warned, "The letter kills, but the Spirit gives life" (2 Cor. 3:6). When Pope John Paul II presented the Pontifical Biblical Commission document *The Interpretation of the Bible in the Church*, he warned his audience about this risk:

A false idea of God and the incarnation presses a certain number of Christians to (...) tend to believe that, since God is the absolute Being, each of his words has an absolute value, independent of all the conditions of human language. Thus, according to them, there is no room for studying these conditions in order to make distinctions that would relativize the significance of the words. However, that is where the illusion occurs and the mysteries of scriptural inspiration and the incarnation are really rejected, by clinging to a false notion of the Absolute. The God of the Bible is not an absolute Being who, crushing everything he touches, would suppress all differences and all nuances. On the contrary, he is God the Creator, who created the astonishing variety of beings "each according to its kind," as the Genesis account says repeatedly (cf. Gen. 1). Far from destroying differences, God respects them and makes use of them (cf. 1 Cor. 12:18, 24, 28). Although he expresses himself in human language, he does not give each expression a uniform value, but uses its possible nuances with extreme flexibility and likewise accepts its limitations.[118]

Fundamentalist non-interpretation of the biblical text goes together with a form of ecclesial community that is sectlike—a closed group with a fortresslike mentality, claiming to defend the truth it thinks it possesses without tolerance for dialogue, other points of view or self-questioning.

I sense that many people really struggle, when they read the Bible, to correlate it with their lives. I think one of the main reasons for this is that so few people have the opportunity to experience *lectio divina* in a community setting—but community is *lectio divina's* native environment. It is where every *lectio* can and should take place. Only within a genuine ecclesial and community context can we breathe life into what is written so that it will rise up as God's living word for us today. The community has hermeneutical power with regard to Scripture. This is why, once again, it would be a very good idea to practice *lectio divina* in parish Bible groups to prepare for the Sunday Eucharistic liturgy. Above all, it is when we are assiduous with Scripture day after day that we come to know how fruitful God's word is, since God never fails to offer the fruits of *lectio* to those who listen faithfully and with love.

CONCLUSION

As a spiritual activity, *lectio divina* will always be challenging and will require sacrifice, discipline, perseverance, and interiorization. Its difficulty makes it an ascetic practice: we need to train ourselves and come back to it regularly.

What each of us personally finds hard is an indicator of what we need to change or work on to grow spiritually to the stature of Christ. The challenges serve a purpose and we can't eliminate them: they are the cost of any encounter, any relationship. The more time we spend with Scripture, the more intensely we will want to know God, be in his presence, hear his word and do his will. We shouldn't be surprised when things become hard: following Christ is not easy!

There is no doubt that the church's future will depend on more people reading the Bible, challenging as it may be. Scripture went through a sort of quarantine in the second millennium, as least for Catholics, but we can hope that the next few decades of this new millennium will be fueled by the energy of the *Dei Verbum*. The "diaspora" situation of Christians today, the fact that we so often find ourselves evaluating Christianity alongside other religions, the need to pray in a more meditative, receptive way: Scripture can guide us in all of these things.

As we give God's word pride of place in our personal lives and communities, we focus on what is essential: allowing the *sequel sancti Evangelii* to give shape to how we live. In the world, in history, wherever people gather, Christians need to make their lives a living exegesis of Scripture, of the Word made flesh.

This is what John Paul II had in mind when, looking at the world like a prophet, he wrote, "To nourish ourselves with the word in order to be 'servants of the word' in the work of evangelization: this is surely a priority for the Church at the dawn of the new millennium."[119]

This is what is at stake in *lectio divina* today.

NOTES

1   Enzo Bianchi, *Praying the Word: An Introduction to Lectio Divina*, trans. James Zona (Kalamazoo, MI: Cistercian Publications, 1998), 67–8.

2   J. Ratzinger, I. de la Potterie, and E. Bianchi, *L'esegesi cristiana oggi* (Casale Monferrato: Piemme, 1991).

3   Origen, *Philokalia* 2:3 (*Philocalie 1-20: Sur les Ecritures*, ed. M. Harl and N. de Lange, SC 302 [Paris: Cerf, 1983]).

4   Ibid., "Introduction."

5   Ibid., 1:28.

6   Origen, *Commentary on the Epistle to the Romans, Books 6-10* (7:17), trans. Thomas P. Scheck (Washington, DC: Catholic University Press, 2002).

7   Ibid.

8   Origen, *Philokalia* 15:19.

9   Origen, *Commentary on the Gospel According to John* 13:5:30.

10 Ibid., 13:5:32.

11 William of Saint-Thierry, *The Golden Epistle: a Letter to the Brethren at Mont Dieu*, 121.

12 A.-M. Pelletier, "Exégèse et histoire: Tirer du nouveau de l'ancien," *Nouvelle Revue Théologique* 110 (1998), 659.

13 Ibid., 663.

14 Henri de Lubac, *Esegesi Medievale I*, Rome: Edizioni Paoline, 1972, 354.

15 C. Theobald, "L'Écriture, âme de la théologie, ou le christianisme comme religion de l'interprétation," in R. Lafontaine et al., *L'Écriture âme de la théologie* (Brussels: Institut d'études théologiques, 1990), 109–132.

16 J. Dupont, "Réflections d'un exégète sur la 'lectio divina' dans la vie du moine," *Liturgie* 60 (1987), 17.

17 P. Guillemette and M. Brisebois, *Introduction aux methods historico-critiques* (Montreal: Fides, 1987), 10.

18 P. Toinet, *Pour une théologie de l'exégèse* (Paris: FAC, 1983), 30.

19 Hugh of Saint-Victor, *Noah's Ark* 2:8, PL 176:642 C–D.

20 *bSanhedrin* 34a, 35a.

21 Zohar III, 202a.

22 *Be-midbar (Numbers) Rabbah* 13:15.

23 Gregory the Great, *Homilies on Ezekiel* 2:9:8.

24 Augustine, *On Christian Teaching* 3:27:38.

25 H. U. von Balthasar, *Con occhi semplici: verso una nuova coscienza cristiana* (Brescia: Herder-Morcelliana, 1970), 19.

26 Louis Bouyer, *Gnosis: la conoscenza di Dio nella Scrittura* (Rome: Libreria Editrice Vaticana, 1991), 10.

27 Cf. H-G. Gadamer, *Truth and Method* (New York: Crossroad, 1985).

28 G. Segalla, "Il 45° congress della 'Studiorum Novi Testamenti Societas' (SNTS) all'Università Cattolica del Sacro Cuore (Milano, 23–27 luglio 1990)," in *Rivista Biblica* 39 (1991), 97.

29 Ibid.

30 Augustine, *On Christian Teaching* 1:36:40.

31 Ibid., 3.15.23.

32   The "unsaid" can be pictured as the white spaces separating
      printed words. The kabbalists speak of the Torah as a single,
      long sentence that goes from "In the beginning" (Gen. 1:1)
      to "all Israel" (Deut. 34:12). If we think of the Hebrew text as
      a long expanse of marks without vocal pointing, accents or
      punctuation, we can understand that the separation of clus-
      ters of consonants to form words and phrases was extremely
      important for comprehension and interpretation. "The radi-
      ance that the white casts on the black letters is itself a source
      of meaning" (Rabbi Levi Isaac of Berditchev, cited in D.
      Banon, *La lecture infinie: Les voies de l'interprétation midrachique* [Paris:
      Seuil, 1987], 118).

33   A. Neher, *L'essenza del profestismo* (Cásale Monferrato: Marietti,
      1984), 95.

34   Ibid., 91; cf. also 73–141.

35   Cf. *Dei Verbum. Genesi della Costituzione sulla divina revelazione:
      Schemi annotate in sinossi*, ed. L. Pacomio (Casale Monferrato:
      Marietti, 1971), 32–133.

36   Origen, *Commentary on the Gospel According to John* 10:30:188.

37   Gaudentius of Brescia, *Second Discourse on Exodus*, PL 20:856A.

38   D. Banon, *La lecture infinie*, 33.

39   *bQiddushin* 30a.

40   A. Milano, *La parola nell'eucharistia: Un approccio storico-teologico*
      (Roma: Dehoniane, 1990), 49.

41   Erveo di Bourg-Dieu, *Commentary on the Letters of St. Paul:
      1 Corinthians 1*, PL 181:824C.

42   M. Magrassi, "Bibbia Pregata," in *L' "oggi" della Parola di Dio nella
      liturgia* (Torino-Leumann: Elledici, 1970), 212.

43　Ambrose of Milan, *Exposition of the Gospel according to Luke* 6:33.

44　Cf. E. Käsemann, "The Pauline Theology of the Cross," in *Interpretation* 24 (1970), 155–156.

45　St. Augustine, *Expositions of the Psalms* 99–120, 103, 4:1, trans. Maria Boulding, osb (Hyde Park, NY: New City Press, 2003), 167.

46　Maximos the Confessor, *Two Hundred Texts on Theology and the Incarnate Dispensation of the Son of God. Written for Thalassios* (2:60), in *The Philokalia*, Vol. II, trans. and ed. G. Palmer, P. Sherrard, and K. Ware (London: Faber and Faber Ltd., 1981), 151.

47　Origen, *Philokalia* 15:19 (SC 302, p. 438).

48　Cf. H. de Lubac, *Esegesi Medievale* I, 325–354.

49　H. U. von Balthasar, "Verbo, Scrittura, Tradizione" in *Saggi Teologici, I. Verbum caro* (Brescia: Morcelliana, 1970), 22.

50　See *Sacrosanctum Concilium* 48 and 51; *Dei Verbum* 26; *Ad Gentes* 6 and 15; *Presbyterorum Ordinis* 18; *Perfectae Caritatis* 6; and especially *Sacrosanctum Concilium* 56 and *Dei Verbum* 21.

51　Ignatius of Antioch, *Letter to the Philadelphians* 4:1.

52　Jerome, *Commentary on Ecclesiastes* 3:12:13.

53　Jerome, *Letters* 22:25.

54　Ambrose of Milan, *I doveri* 1:20:88, ed. G. Banterle (Milan-Rome: Biblioteca Ambrosiana-Città Nuova, 1977), 77.

55　Deuteronomy 8:2–3, Amos 8:11, Jeremiah 15:16, Psalms 119 and 103, Wisdom 16:26, Sirach 24:18–22, Proverbs 9:1–5, Ezekiel 3:3, Matthew 4:4, Revelation 10:9, etc.

56　Jerome, *Commentary on Matthew* 1:4:4.

57　Origen, *Homilies on Numbers* 3:1:1.

58　Origen, *Commentary on the Gospel of Matthew: Fragments* 218.

59   Rupert of Deutz, *On the Trinity* 3 and *On the Holy Spirit* 1:6.

60   "Corpus Christi intelligitur etiam Scriptura Dei" (Cited in H. de Lubac, *Esegesi Medievale II* [Milan: Jaca Book, 1998], 166).

61   Origen, *Commentary on Matthew: Series* 85 (ed. G. Bendinelli et al [Rome: Città Nuova, 2006, vol. II], 93).

62   Jerome, *Commentary on Psalm* 147.

63   Origen, *Commentary on the Gospel of Matthew* 11:14.

64   Cf. H. de Lubac, *Storia e spirito* (Milan: Jaca Book, 1985), 385–403.

65   Cf. Origen, *Homilies on Leviticus* 7:5.

66   Ambrose of Milan, *Commentary on the Psalms* 1:83.

67   Rupert of Deutz, *Commentary on the Gospel of John* 6:11b.

68   Cf. E. Bianchi, *Dall'ascolto della Parola alla preghiera liturgica* (Bose: Qiqajon, 1990), (Testi di meditazione 33).

69   Gregory the Great, *Homilies on Ezekiel* 2:4:19.

70   E. Ruffini, "Sacramentalità ed economia sacramentale negli scritti dei padre della chiesa," in E. Ruffini and E. Lodi, *"Mysterion" e "sacramentum": La sacramentalità negli scritti dei padre e nei testi liturgici primitivi* (Bologna: EDB, 1987), 189.

71   "Per cor Christi intelligitur Sacra Scriptura quae manifestat cor Christi" (Thomas Aquinas, *Commentary on the Psalms* 21:11).

72   *Discorsi di Massimo IV al Concilio: Discorsi e note del patriarca Massimo IV e dei vescovi della sua chiesa al Concilio ecumenico Vaticano II* (Bologna: EDB, 1968), 63.

73   J.-P. Sonnet, "Figures (anciennes et nouvelles) du lecteur: Du Cantique des Cantiques au Livre entier," in *Nouvelle Revue Théologique* 113 (1991), 85.

74   A.-M. Pelletier, *Lectures du Cantique des Cantiques* (Rome: Editrice Pontificio Istituto Biblico, 1989), 420.

75   J. A. Sanders, *Identité de la Bible: Torah et canon* (Paris: Cerf, 1975), 151.

76   F.-P. Dreyfus, "Exégèse en Sorbonne, exégèse en Église," 353.

77   Origen, *Homilies on Genesis* 7:2.

78   Origen, *Homilies on Numbers* 11:1:10.

79   Augustine, *Commentary on the Gospel of John* 24:7.

80   Hilary of Poitiers, *Commentary on the Psalms* 54:2.

81   Bernard of Clairvaux, *Sermon 57: On Easter* 2.

82   Gregory the Great, *Homilies on Ezekiel* I:7:17.

83   Ignatius of Antioch, *Epistle to the Philadelphians* Ch. 8 (The Ante-Nicene Fathers, Vol. 1 [Edinburgh, UK, and Grand Rapids, MI: T&T Clark/Eerdmans, 1989]).

84   Origen, *Commentary on the Gospel of Matthew* 14:4.

85   Augustine, *Expositions of the Psalms* 105:36.

86   Origen, *Commentary on the Gospel of John* 1:4:23.

87   *Commentary on the Psalms* 68, PG 12:1516C (attributed to Evagrius Ponticus).

88   Cf. Augustine, *On Christian Teaching* 2:12:17.

89   Gregory the Great, *Homilies on Ezekiel* II:2:1.

90   John Cassian, *Conferences* 10:11.

91   P. Ricoeur, "Esquisse de conclusion," in R. Barthes et al., *Exégèse et herméneutique*, 295.

92   b.Berakhot 61b.

93   J. Leclercq, *The Love of Learning and the Desire for God*, trans. C. Misrahi (New York: Fordham University Press, 1982), 15.

94 J.-P. Sonnet, *La parole consacrée: Théorie des actes de langage, linguistique de l'énonciation et parole de la foi* (Louvain: Cabay, 1984), 98.

95 Thomas Aquinas, *Summa Theologica* III, q. 62, a.5.

96 John Chrysostom, *Homilies on Genesis* 37:1, PG 53:341.

97 Clement of Rome, *Letter to the Corinthians* 45:2.

98 Hilary of Poitiers, *Commentary on Psalm 118*.

99 Cf. Acts 28:25 (with reference to Isa. 6:9–10), Hebrews 3:7 (with reference to Ps. 95:7–11), Hebrews 10:15–17 (with reference to Jer. 31:33–34), etc.

100 Spoken by Rabbi Ishmael in *Sifre Numbers* 15:31.

101 Origen, *Homilies on Leviticus* 4:1.

102 M.-J. Rondeau, "Actualité de l'éxègese patristique?", in *Les quatre fleuves* 7 (1977), 98.

103 Rashi of Troyes, *Commentary on Exodus* 19:1.

104 Augustine, *On Christian Teaching* 3:37:56.

105 Guigo II the Carthusian, *The Ladder of Monks* 2, trans. Edmund Colledge and James Walsh (Kalamazoo, MI: Cistercian Publications, 1981), 68.

106 "Te totum applica ad textum; rem totam applica ad te" (J.A. Bengel, 1687–1752, in the Preface to his 1734 edition of the Greek New Testament).

107 Athanasius of Alexandria, *Letter to the Bishops of Africa* 4, PG 26:1036A.

108 Augustine, *Discourses* LVI:6:10.

109 Origen is especially fond of this theme: see his *Commentary on the Gospel of Matthew*.

110 Bernard of Clairvaux, *On the Song of Songs IV* (74:5), trans. Irene Edmonds (Kalamazoo, MI: Cistercian Publications, 1980), 89–90.

111 John Paul II, *Novo Millennio Ineunte* 39.

112 Cf. Enzo Bianchi, *Dall'ascolto della Parola alla preghiera liturgica,* and *L'essere povero come condizione essenziale per leggere la Bibbia.* See also Enzo Bianchi, "Lectio divina et vie monastique," in *La Vie Spirituelle* 714 (1995), 145–159.

113 J. Ratzinger, in *Consilium Conferentiarum Episcoporum Europae,* Rome 2001.

114 Gregory the Great, *Homilies on Ezekiel* 1:17:8.

115 Cf. I. Illich, *Du lisible au visible: la naissance du texte. Un commentaire du "Didascalicon" de Hugues de Saint-Victor* (Paris: Cerf, 1991), 9.

116 P. Ricoeur, *Essays on Biblical Interpretation* (Philadelphia: Fortress, 1980), 105–108.

117 L. Alonso-Schökel, "È attuale il linguaggio del Vecchio Testamento? (cap. IV della *Dei Verbum*)," in S. Lyonnet et al., *La Bibbia nella Chiesa dopo la "Dei Verbum." Studi sulla costituzione conciliare* (Roma: Edizioni Paoline, 1969), 117.

118 Text available online: http://archive.salvationhistory.com /library/scripture/churchandbible/pastoral/pope93.cfm2.htm (accessed March 15, 2014).

119 John Paul II, *Novo millennio ineunte* 40.

ABOUT PARACLETE PRESS

WHO WE ARE

Paraclete Press is a publisher of books, recordings, and DVDs on Christian spirituality. Our publishing represents a full expression of Christian belief and practice—from Catholic to Evangelical, from Protestant to Orthodox.

We are the publishing arm of the Community of Jesus, an ecumenical monastic community in the Benedictine tradition. As such, we are uniquely positioned in the marketplace without connection to a large corporation and with informal relationships to many branches and denominations of faith.

WHAT WE ARE DOING

Paraclete Press Books

Paraclete publishes books that show the richness and depth of what it means to be Christian. Although Benedictine spirituality is at the heart of all that we do, we publish books that reflect the Christian experience across many cultures, time periods, and houses of worship. We publish books that nourish the vibrant life of the church and its people.

We have several different series, including the best-selling Paraclete Essentials and Paraclete Giants series of classic texts in contemporary English; Voices from the Monastery—men and women monastics writing about living a spiritual life today; award-winning poetry; best-selling gift books for children on the occasions of baptism and first communion; and the Active Prayer Series that brings creativity and liveliness to any life of prayer.

Mount Tabor Books

Paraclete's newest series, Mount Tabor Books, focuses on liturgical worship, art and art history, ecumenism, and the first millennium church, and was created in conjunction with the Mount Tabor Ecumenical Centre for Art and Spirituality in Barga, Italy.

Paraclete Recordings

From Gregorian chant to contemporary American choral works, our recordings celebrate the best of sacred choral music composed through the centuries that create a space for heaven and earth to intersect. Paraclete Recordings is the record label representing the internationally acclaimed choir Gloriæ Dei Cantores, praised for their "rapt and fathomless spiritual intensity" by *American Record Guide*; the Gloriæ Dei Cantores Schola, specializing in the study and performance of Gregorian chant; and the other instrumental artists of the Gloriæ Dei Artes Foundation.

Paraclete Press is also privileged to be the exclusive North American distributor of the recordings of the Monastic Choir of St. Peter's Abbey in Solesmes, France, long considered to be a leading authority on Gregorian chant.

Paraclete Video Productions

Our DVDs offer spiritual help, healing, and biblical guidance for a broad range of life issues including grief and loss, marriage, forgiveness, facing death, bullying, addictions, Alzheimer's, and spiritual formation.

Learn more about us at our website:
www.paracletepress.com or phone us
toll-free at 1.800.451.5006

SCAN
TO
READ
MORE

Other titles by modern monastics available from
Paraclete Press…

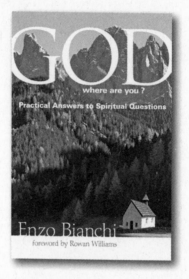

GOD, WHERE ARE YOU?
Practical Answers to Spiritual Questions
ENZO BIANCHI

ISBN: 978-1-61261-574-5, $16.99, Paperback

Enzo Bianchi helps us finds God in stories from the Old Testament: stories of Abraham, Jacob, and Moses. It is the divine within us who really poses the question, "God, where are you?" When we truly begin to search for God, we discover that not only is God real, but He is already looking for us!

ECHOES OF THE WORD
A New Kind of Monk on the Meaning of Life
ENZO BIANCHI

ISBN: 978-1-61261-373-4, $15.99, Paperback

A t the heart of the book is the conviction that life has meaning: it is not our task to invent or determine that meaning but simply to discover it—present and active—in and around us.

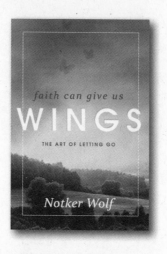